# TALES OF FREEDOM

To Rosie,
With love
xxx Maggie a Isabel
2000 – 2001

VESSANTARA

# TALES OF FREEDOM

*Wisdom from the Buddhist Tradition*

WINDHORSE PUBLICATIONS

*Also by Vessantara:*
Meeting the Buddhas
The Mandala of the Five Buddhas


Published by Windhorse Publications
11 Park Road
Birmingham
B13 8AB

Cover design Vincent Stokes
Cover image © Getty Images
Printed by Interprint Ltd, Marsa, Malta

*A catalogue record for this book is available from the British Library*

ISBN 1 899579 27 3

*The publishers acknowledge with gratitude permission to quote from the following:*

pp.31, 37, 44. We quote by permission of the Pali Text Society which owns the copyright in the work *Poems of Early Buddhist Nuns (Therīgāthā),* trans. Mrs C.A.F. Rhys Davids and K.R. Norman, Pali Text Society, Oxford 1989. The author has incorporated his own adaptations of this translation.

pp.98–9. Reproduced by permission of Oxford University Press from Herbert V. Guenther (trans.), *The Life and Teaching of Nāropa,* © Oxford University Press, 1963.

p.143. D.T. Suzuki, *Essays in Zen Buddhism,* Rider, 1977.

p.155. Trevor Leggett (trans.), *The Tiger's Cave – Translations of Japanese Texts,* Routledge and Kegan Paul, 1977.

# CONTENTS

## About the Author

Vessantara is a senior member of the Western Buddhist Order. Born Tony McMahon in London in 1950, he gained an MA in English at Cambridge University. Interested in Buddhism since his teens, he first had direct contact with Buddhists in 1971. In 1974 he became a member of the Western Buddhist Order and was given the name Vessantara, which means 'universe within'.

In 1975 he gave up a career in social work to become chairman of the Brighton Buddhist Centre. Since then he has divided his time between meditating, studying Buddhism, and aiding the development of several Buddhist centres, including retreat centres in England, Wales, and Spain. During the 1980s he led seven three-month courses for people entering the Order. For six years he was secretary to Sangharakshita, the founder of the Order. In 1994 he was asked by Sangharakshita to be one of the group of senior disciples to whom he was passing on overall responsibility for the Buddhist movement he had founded.

Whilst drawing on the whole Buddhist tradition for inspiration, Vessantara has a particular love for Tibetan Buddhism. In 1993 he published *Meeting the Buddhas* – a richly illustrated introduction to the Buddhas, Bodhisattvas, and tantric deities that are meditated upon within the Tibetan tradition.

He is much in demand as a teacher, giving talks and leading retreats and workshops in Europe, the USA, and Australasia. He is known particularly as a storyteller, and this book draws on some of his favourite incidents from the different Buddhist traditions.

## Acknowledgements

Like everything else in life, a book appears as the result of a very complex network of conditions. Many people have consciously or unwittingly played their part in bringing this one into existence, from the audiences on whom I first tried out these stories to the proofreader of the final text. Many thanks to those who transcribed the talks on which most of this book is based, and to all those who read drafts and gave comments. I'm particularly grateful to Jnana-garbha for his help with the story in Chapter 1.

It has been a pleasure to work with the people at Windhorse Publications again. Jan Parker was a very helpful editor in the early phase of the project. Sara Hagel subsequently took over this role, and has been an encouraging friend and discerning critic. Padmavajri, Shantavira, and Dhivati have taken their usual great care to ensure that the final product was clear, spruce, and on time.

Seen from a wider perspective, the chain of conditions for the arising of this book stretches back far into the past. It includes all those who have kept these stories alive by retelling them, orally or in writing. I would like to express my particular thanks to Trevor Leggett, a fine story-teller, through whose efforts I first became aware of the Zen stories on which my last three chapters are based.

To the above, and to the many friends who have encouraged me to keep writing, I offer my heartfelt thanks.

*Vessantara, Birmingham, England*
*7 May 2000*

# Preface

Once upon a time there was a man who was deeply happy. He was not bothered by the prospect of growing old or being ill; he had no fear of dying. He lived free as a bird, contentedly wandering from place to place, unconcerned by being far from his family, with no money at all, and sometimes not even having anything to eat. He never did a day's work in his life. He had nothing to do except to enjoy his freedom and teach people that he met the secret of becoming free themselves.

Put that way, it sounds like a folk tale or fairy story. However, that paragraph is a fair summary of the life of a historical figure, the Buddha, from the time of his Enlightenment until his death at the age of 80. I could write similar true stories about many thousands of his male and female disciples down through the centuries, who followed his directions to arrive at states of inner freedom and fulfilment. This book deals with stories of real people, and is an attempt in a small way to carry on doing what the Buddha did, teaching people how to be free.

There are now thousands of books about Buddhism available to us in the West. Many of them explain the Buddha's teaching in rational terms. However, in this book I have focused on telling stories to illustrate the Buddhist path to freedom. Buddhism is a path of self-transformation in which both head and heart have to be deeply engaged. Thus it has always spoken to the imagination and the emotions as well as the intellect. In fact the best Buddhist teaching does both. That is the wonder of a story. We can live through it in imagination; we can feel for the characters. When a good story is well told to some extent it is as if the events have happened to us, and it has its impact on our lives, on who we are.

In each chapter you will find a main story and then a commentary upon it, drawing out aspects of the Buddhist understanding of life. My comments are far from being the final word on the stories. However, they do at least provide ways to help you explore their significance. If your knowledge of Buddhism is limited they will also give you the basic information you need in order to understand their context. All the Buddhist stories are presented as being true by their traditional sources, which are given in the Notes at the end of the book. I have tried to be faithful to those sources, while using a storyteller's licence to fill in details to bring the stories alive.

I have told many stories in my Buddhist teaching over the years. For this book I have chosen some personal favourites. They are also ones which people have told me they found particularly useful for them in their search for freedom under the circumstances of modern life in the West. Before we look at the inspiring stories which are to come, in Chapter 1 we encounter a contemporary tale, which illustrates with chilling clarity the effects of failing to follow the path to freedom, and in particular the suffering we can cause – to ourselves and others – when we ignore the ethical dimension of life. The rest of the stories are taken from three of the main traditions of Buddhism. Those in Part Two are drawn from the Pāli Canon, which is preserved in the Theravada Buddhist tradition of South-East Asia. In Part Three we enter the rich world of Tibetan Buddhism, as well as meeting Nāropa, an Indian guru whose teachings had a great impact on the development of Buddhism in Tibet. Finally, in Part Four we travel to Japan, to watch three Zen Buddhist teachers dealing with life-threatening situations.

All the Buddhist stories convey a sense of deep inner freedom, and give pointers to how we can develop it in our own lives. Just what that inner freedom involves, and how it can be achieved, should become increasingly clear the more of these stories you read. Each chapter fills in a part of the picture. To generalize very broadly, the first chapter outlines the factors which prevent us from being free; the Pāli Canon stories show us ordinary people working to liberate themselves from limiting feelings such as grief, guilt and anger; the Tibetan chapters demonstrate how one can overcome the sense of existential isolation; and the Zen chapters describe ways of retaining freedom even in the face of death.

Thus all the stories are, in their different ways, 'tales of freedom' which will provide us with keys to unlocking the steel doors of ignorance and negative emotions which stand between us and freedom. In fact, if we take them to heart, they will provide us with an understanding which will enable us to walk through the walls of our own self-constructed mental prisons and roam free in the vast space of the nature of Reality.

# PART ONE

# How Freedom Disappears

# 1

## All at Sea

### A Cautionary Tale

We are most motivated to do something when we are both pushed and pulled – pushed by seeing the unpleasant consequences if we do not do it; pulled by the delights awaiting us if we do. This is definitely true of following the path to freedom. Nearly all the stories in this book describe men and women winning their freedom, or acting in ways which demonstrate how a human being can be free even under the most difficult circumstances. Hopefully they will inspire us with a vision of how we could live, who we could become.

However, this first story is not a tale of freedom. It does not feature any Buddhist practitioner with the light of wisdom in their eyes. In fact it is a cautionary tale, a warning of the natural outcome of losing our grip on truth, until we find we have no freedom left at all. It is a true story about events which happened quite recently, but it has much of the hair-raising quality and ethical implications of a Greek tragedy. It struck me very forcefully when I first heard it, and it has affected me ever since. Reflecting on it always gives me a push in the direction of freedom.

### The Lone Sailor

It is 1968, and in the Somerset town of Bridgwater the owner of Electron Utilisation is worried. Donald Crowhurst is in his mid-thirties, married, with four children. Electron Utilisation makes electronic components for self-steering yacht equipment, and it is heading for the rocks. In the face of all his concerns about bankruptcy, and the loss of social standing this would cause, Crowhurst's main form of respite is sailing.

Only the previous year Sir Francis Chichester has become a national hero after his solo voyage around the world. This has made single-handed sailing and racing quite fashionable, and the *Sunday Times* has sponsored a competition – the Golden Globe Race. This is a single-handed yacht race around the world, with a prize of £5,000. It seems to Crowhurst that this might be the way out of his difficulties. He is a good, although not expert, sailor. If he were to enter the race he might be able to get some sponsorship, as well as some good publicity for his business. If he were to win, or even to finish well up the field, it might be enough to solve his problems.

Before long Crowhurst has acquired a boat which he has named Teignmouth Electron – 'Teignmouth' after his port of departure and 'Electron' after his business. He has persuaded people to sponsor him, and to donate much of the equipment and materials he will need on his voyage. He even has a press officer, an ebullient character called Rodney Hallworth.

The Golden Globe Race has no starting line; the winner will be the person who takes the least time in their circumnavigation: round Africa, past Australia, round Cape Horn, and back to England. People set off at different times, and whoever has the shortest elapsed time between their departure and their return will win. However, there is a deadline by which competitors have to start, and Crowhurst has left it late. Right up to the last minute he is stuffing things into his unfinished boat in Teignmouth. The cabin is littered with tins of food and all the other things he needs to survive, including bits of electronic gear which he hasn't had time to put together. Hallworth is busily feeding the press with titbits about how things are going, as Crowhurst hurries around saying goodbye to his friends and family. Finally, on 31 October, he waves farewell to his wife, and sails off.

To begin with he is very busy getting the boat organized, and starting work on the electronic equipment. Teignmouth Electron is a trimaran and should be capable of sailing fast, at least before the wind. However, it quickly becomes clear that, because of the rush to meet the starting deadline, the boat has a number of very worrying faults. Several of the safety features do not work, his self-steering gear is not fully functional, and some of the hatches are leaking.

Then, as he sails south along the coast of Africa, he runs into some violent weather, and in this very first storm his boat fares badly. Nursing it through heavy seas and buffeting winds is very demanding, but eventually the weather calms down and Crowhurst sits off the coast of Africa, contemplating his situation. He has plenty of time to think about it because he is on his own in the ocean with nothing around. He is trying to work out the chances of being able to make it all the way round the world in this ill-prepared boat. If he cannot do it where does that leave him? It leaves him with a business on the rocks and all kinds of expenses and difficulties. What is he to do? He is not going to gain any publicity out of sailing a little way down the coast of Africa, and then limping out of the race.

Crowhurst begins working on repairs, and moves out of the main trade routes to avoid being run down by shipping. He records all this in the yacht's log: a record of position, speed of progress, radio communications, and any notable events.

We don't quite know when it starts, and we don't quite know if, in the beginning, it was just a fantasy and a way of keeping himself amused because he had so much time to fill. When you are on your own in the middle of an ocean there is plenty of time for thinking. At some point one of the ideas he plays with is that of starting another log. He begins writing an imaginary log, an account of what would have happened, where he would be if his boat had not been damaged, if he had carried on making the same rate of progress. He would be well down the coast of Africa, really beginning to make inroads into his circumnavigation. Meanwhile, in the original log of reality he is drifting along, trying to put his boat back together again, making very little progress.

Even if it did start off as a piece of wish-fulfilment to help pass the time, at some point this new log in which he is doing very well begins to take on a new meaning. A plan comes to him by which he might still save his business and position. What he has to do is to *appear* to have gone most of the way round the world, and then reappear at the right time coming up through the western Atlantic, heading back towards Britain. Instead of having to go all the way around Africa, Australia, and Cape Horn, he can just waste months and months meandering around somewhere in the South Atlantic. He will have to make sure that he stays out of the shipping lanes so that nobody sees him. Then, when a suitable amount of time has passed, he can reappear, re-enter the race, and come in somewhere down the field. In this way he would appear to do fairly well, and his press agent could make something of his finishing in a creditable position.

There is just one problem: all the competitors are supposed to make radio contact as they sail past Sydney, and Crowhurst will not be going within an ocean of Australia....

With so much time on his hands it isn't long before he thinks of a way around this conundrum. If there were something wrong with his generator he would be unable to make contact with Sydney. He promptly sends off a message: he is having problems with his generator; people should not expect to hear from him for a long time; he will work on it and maybe at some point he will be able to repair it, but he's not sure. After sending this message he has time to kill. Months to kill. And now he is completely isolated; he cannot even use his radio. It is as if he has to die for a few months, and then re-emerge into the race at the right moment.

Rodney Hallworth has managed to interest the BBC in Crowhurst, so they have given him a film camera and a tape recorder. He films himself sitting on the boat, talking about this and that, about how he is finding life, his diet, fish and birds he has seen, and how he is spending his time. He fills many hours in this way. He also spends much time keeping his logs – not only of where he is but also of where he would like to be. He needs to work out what would be reasonable progress all the way through his long hypothetical journey around the world. He works hard on that, but still keeps his other log stating what he is actually doing. In the invented log he is passing the Cape of Good Hope, then crossing the Indian Ocean, heading for Australia. In the real log he is in the South Atlantic, going nowhere. Time passes, and he is left with his thoughts. For months he is in solitary confinement in the tiny, rolling cell of the Teignmouth Electron.

Having committed himself to this deception, he still has other worries. His boat has so many leaks and other faults that he cannot be entirely sure it will make it back to England. Eventually he decides that if he is to have any chance of completing his voyage, he will have to put into a port somewhere and find supplies. With just a few bits and pieces he can do the work on the boat so that when the time comes he can return to England. Eventually he puts in to the smallest fishing port he can find, Rio Salado in Argentina, acquires the things he needs, and sets off again. This gives him another worry, because one of the stipulations of the race is that it must be an unassisted circumnavigation. If anyone were to find out that a small craft with an Englishman aboard had put in and been given supplies he would be disqualified. Not only that, it would prove him to be thousands of miles away from where he is supposed to be, so he has that to worry about too. He still cannot use the radio because that would blow his cover. He is completely on his own, drifting around the South Atlantic with time to kill and nothing happening....

But gradually the months do pass. He is still in the South Atlantic, and beginning to think about heading back towards England. He has not used his radio for eleven weeks. It is time for him to make radio contact, and find out what has been happening in the race. He discovers that his press officer, Hallworth, has been tearing his hair out. Without any word from Crowhurst, with nothing to work with or feed the newspapers, he has had to improvise. He has painted Crowhurst as the dark horse of the race who, before he lost radio contact, was making very good time, and who could well be up among the leaders.

Worryingly for Crowhurst it transpires that he *is* among the leaders! The weather, the strain, and the isolation have taken their toll on the other competitors, and out of the original starters there are now only four left. In addition to Crowhurst, there is Robin Knox-Johnston, ex-Royal Navy, who is back in England, safe and dry, but his elapsed time from departure to return is quite long. He started off early and went very steadily, and so far he is the only person to have completed the course. There is also another Englishman, a naval officer called Nigel Tetley, who has made quite good time and is now most of the way back to England. Then there is the race leader: a Frenchman, Bernard Moitessier. He is a very unusual character, a kind of mystic of the sea. He is not really bothered about winning; he just loves sailing; he is fulfilled by being out on the ocean, pitting himself against it, giving everything that it demands of him. Although he is not yet back in Europe he is well out in front, and obviously going to win. And now the dark horse of the race, Donald Crowhurst, has reappeared. He has radioed his position as having rounded Cape Horn and coming into the Atlantic, which leaves him about equal second. Moitessier is well out in front, then Tetley more or less neck-and-neck with Crowhurst, and lastly Knox-Johnston, back home in England, but whose time is the slowest by far.

Once Crowhurst has received a cable from Hallworth and learnt all this news he needs some time to reflect. He thinks hard about the fact that he is going to come second or third. This might well be more publicity than he wants. The log of his imaginary circumnavigation will really have to stand up to scrutiny if he ends up amongst the top finishers. People will be interested in his achievement, and how he managed it. He decides to take his time in his journey towards England, because third place would be less high-profile than second. He sails back towards England at a leisurely pace, keeping in radio contact as he goes.

Sometimes it seems that the fates are against us, and while Crowhurst loiters in the Atlantic there are other forces at play. A little while later Crowhurst makes contact with England again and hears dramatic news. Moitessier, the mystic man of the sea, has decided not to return to Europe. His love of sailing is so deep that he doesn't care about the Golden Globe Race, about any race, prize money, or fame. His enjoyment of single-handedly sailing around the world is so great that he sets out on another circuit. He sails out of the race, away on his own mystic quest.

Hallworth is naturally gleeful, but Crowhurst, though having to appear jubilant, is far from delighted with the news. This development leaves him in second place. His only solace is that he is not first. If he were to win he would be the centre of attention; the records of his journey would be keenly inspected. That wasn't what he had set out to do: he just wanted to come in fairly anonymously, somewhere down the field, to gain a little publicity so that he could avoid going bankrupt and keep his kids at school. He sails anxiously on towards England, brooding on what to do.

It seems that Nigel Tetley (the English naval officer who is now about equal first with Crowhurst) has been having some reflections himself. He had been heading for home, knowing there was no way he could beat Moitessier, but thinking he was assured of second place, being well ahead of Knox-Johnston's time. All of a sudden, out of nowhere, this weekend sailor Donald Crowhurst has appeared on his tail, making as good time as he is. When Moitessier sails out of the race, he and Crowhurst are neck and neck for the first prize. His naval pride is at stake, and he determines to do his best to ensure that he comes in first. Urged on by his supporters, he presses on as fast as he possibly can. He keeps pushing his boat to its limits to beat Crowhurst, even when he runs into a storm near the Azores. As a result, on 21 May 1969, Nigel Tetley is winched out of the Atlantic into a helicopter. The remains of his boat are little more than driftwood, and he is out of the race. This leaves Donald Crowhurst sailing back to Teignmouth to a hero's welcome, as Hallworth is now enthusiastically telling him. A naval minesweeper will escort him into port, past the banner reading 'Teignmouth welcomes Crowhurst', with BBC and ITN helicopters overhead. As he lands he will be met by the chairman of Teignmouth Council to receive a formal civic welcome. The *Sunday Times* will lay on a car to drive him up to London, where there will be a press conference, receptions, a banquet. He will be guest of honour, seated next to Sir Francis Chichester. The two of them will be able to swap their experiences of going round Cape Horn.

Crowhurst's heart sinks. He is still keeping his two logs. There is the one where he went round Cape Horn: the gales, the huge waves, the struggle and danger. Then there is the one in which he has simply been meandering around, and he has been no nearer to Cape Horn than the Falkland Islands. He has been sailing with nowhere to go, and he has been on his own for so long now. He speaks to his wife on the radio, 'Are you all right at home? Are you sure you can cope with all the difficulties?' His proud wife reassures him that she is coping, and that he need not think of pulling out of the race on her account.

What is he to do? He can't go back to England, and sail into Teignmouth with all the bunting and the cheering crowds, the reception committees and the media. He can't go to London to talk to Sir Francis Chichester about a trip round Cape Horn that he never made. But what other option is there? He can't just sail around for ever. There's the business. And his wife. The children. Hallworth. All those people. Whichever of his logs he reads, they both bring him back to the same impossible position.

He is keeping a diary, and at this point Donald Crowhurst begins to record what he believes are new truths. The tone of the diary keeps tacking between depression and elated 'understandings' about Einstein, God, the nature of the universe. Out of these increasingly wild swings, Crowhurst comes to believe that the truth of his journey is that he has been playing a game of chess. A game of chess with God, or perhaps the Devil. And now his position is desperate. In fact there doesn't seem to be any way out. It is time to resign.

Ten days pass with no further communication from Crowhurst. On 11 July 1969, nearly eight-and-a-half months after its departure, Teignmouth Electron is found by a British freighter, still heading towards England in a gentle swell. But Donald Crowhurst is no longer on board. There is no sign of him anywhere.

### *Blowing a Gale From Eight Directions*

So that is my cautionary tale.[1] In the rest of this chapter we shall explore it to see what it can teach us about freedom and the human condition. It is a shocking story, because we can see so clearly the consequences of what starts out as quite a small deception. Step by step, Crowhurst is moved into a position from which it seems increasingly impossible to escape. Although the story shows us an extreme, it is moving because – in a way – there is nothing special about Donald Crowhurst at all. He has normal human concerns – his wife, his children, making ends meet – which do not usually lead to such tragic consequences. It is clear enough that it was his willingness to depart from the truth and keep two logs which led Crowhurst inexorably to his fate. If we analyse what happened, we see that he was led to do this by some unhelpful motivations which are also at play in us. Looking at their catastrophic results in Crowhurst's case can help us see their more subtle damaging effects on our own lives. These everyday motivations all cause us unwittingly to give up our freedom. They are known in the Buddhist tradition as the 'eight worldly winds'. In Crowhurst's case they blew his life right off course, and finally shipwrecked it altogether.

The eight worldly winds consist of four pairs of opposites, of which one is pleasant and agreeable, the other unpleasant and usually avoided. The first pair is gain and loss. In Crowhurst's case he was worried that he was about to become bankrupt. His voyage was an attempt to rescue his struggling business, to preserve his family's standard of living, to enable him to continue giving his children a good education. When his boat was damaged early in the race, the winds of gain and loss prevented him from accepting what had happened. He gambled that by lying he could rescue himself and his family from ruin.

Secondly, there are praise and blame. These also encouraged Crowhurst to paint himself into a corner. There were people close to him who had had misgivings about his lack of experience, his rushed preparations, the risks of using a fast but possibly unstable trimaran design. Crowhurst was always a self-reliant adventurer, prepared to back his ideas and opinions. It would not have been easy for him to have withdrawn from the race, and to have people saying 'I told you so....'

Thirdly, there are fame and infamy or notoriety. Crowhurst does not seem to have courted fame, although he obviously took a certain pride in projecting an image of himself for the BBC camera he had on board. However, Crowhurst eventually faced the possibility, if the truth came out, of being known by millions of people around the world as the cheat who had attempted to fool the judges in the *Sunday Times* race. How many of us could cope with the notoriety of being exposed as a liar and fraud in front not only of our family or even of everyone in our local town, but of the world's media? (Although it has to be said that some people would love to be famous, to be a celebrity, even for negative reasons. They feel jealous and deprived if they have never had their fifteen minutes in the artificial sun of the television spotlights. Perhaps in our media-conscious age the opposite of fame is no longer notoriety but obscurity.)

Lastly, and most basic of all, there are pleasure and pain. This pair underlies all the other sets of opposites. They goad us through all our waking hours, as our nervous system constantly responds to stimuli, inner and outer. Indeed, if we let them, all four pairs prevent us from ever being at peace. They rule our lives and deprive us of our freedom. Naturally, pleasure and pain had their hold on Crowhurst. Indeed, the pain of the loss, blame, and notoriety which he would face prevented him from admitting the truth to anyone, and finally prevented him returning at all.

However, speaking in this way puts the problem 'out there', when the difficulty lies not with praise, blame, and so forth in themselves, but with how we deal with them. The worldly winds blow us around because we respond to them with craving and aversion. We are led on by craving for pleasure, gain, praise, and fame, except for the times when we are on the run, driven by our aversion to pain, loss, blame, and notoriety. As a result, most people steer an unsteady course through life, a course largely determined by their responses to the varying strengths of the eight winds acting upon them. Sadly, this was the case with Donald Crowhurst. Teignmouth Electron was damaged but survived the storms. It was the gales of the worldly winds swirling about Crowhurst, increasing in strength over the months, which finally blew him overboard.

### Siddhārtha and Liberation from the Eight Winds

How are we to avoid becoming controlled by the eight winds? Siddhārtha, the historical Buddha, was faced with this question in a very stark form. In the early part of his life the winds breathed on him as seductive breezes. As the son of a leading figure in society he led a very hedonistic life. He lived in luxury: in palaces with musicians and dancing girls to entertain him. He was fit and strong, successful in archery and other competitions. According to some texts, he was married to a beautiful woman, and had a young son. He was known throughout the Sākyan state, and people had high hopes for him as someone who would one day have great power and influence.

However, despite having a life that many people would envy, Siddhārtha was deeply dissatisfied. He saw that pleasure, riches, praise, and renown were all enticing mirages, and that beyond them lurked the shades of sickness, old age, and death. So he gave up basing his life on the pursuit of these mirages, left home, and went wandering from place to place in pursuit of truth and freedom. Joining some ascetic yogis who believed that practising austerities was the way to freedom, Siddhārtha deliberately courted the four winds that most people avoid. He fasted, went naked, and pushed himself to extremes of suffering. He spent six years in these grim pursuits, becoming renowned for his self-mortification, before finally deciding that asceticism was a dead end, and that he was no freer than before.

By giving up asceticism he had to suffer his admirers' disappointment and rejection. He was left completely alone. Far from making him give up his quest for freedom, the failure of asceticism to satisfy him made him even more determined. He began reflecting deeply on the human condition. It began to dawn on him that the path to freedom involved not allowing oneself to be controlled by pleasure or pain. He started taking care of his body and enjoying his experience, but he did not fall into the trap of returning to the hedonism of his early years. Similarly, he no longer sought out pain, but when it was unavoidable he accepted it. He began practising meditation, in a determined but relaxed way. However, he avoided the tendency to crave for and cling to pleasure. As a result, he entered states of deeply blissful concentration, yet, as he recounted later, 'I allowed no such pleasant feeling as arose in me to gain power over my mind.'[2]

From the vantage point of deeply concentrated and serene meditative states, Siddhārtha was able to look more clearly at life than ever before. Finally, seated under a tree by the banks of the Neranjara River, he gained the state of complete Enlightenment. During this experience he came to many realizations. He recognized the fact that all phenomena arise in dependence upon conditions. He saw that all conditioned existence is impermanent and can never give permanent fulfilment. He understood that the sense that we all have of being a fixed, inherently-existing self, an 'I' standing behind or apart from, and somehow controlling, the mind and body, is an illusion. He experienced the fact that in reality there is no fixed 'I', only the ceaseless flow of events that make up our mental and physical experience. Similarly, he experienced the unreality of his sense of being confronted with an external world made up of fixed entities. He knew directly that all experience is open-ended. In this illuminating vision of the true nature of things, even the idea of being a fixed subject relating to a separate external world collapsed, and Siddhārtha experienced an interconnectedness with all life. Out of that flowed a deep love and compassion for all living beings.

Siddhārtha did not experience these things just as ideas. He saw the truth that they embody, directly and intuitively, in a way that completely transformed him. As a result, he arrived at a state of complete inner freedom. Thus he became known as the Buddha, which literally means 'one who has awakened'.

Liberated by his deep insight into the impermanent and conditioned nature of all experience, and the illusoriness of an inherently-existent self, the Buddha no longer based his life on hopes and fears connected with the eight worldly winds. In the traditional phrase, he found a Middle Way between hedonism and asceticism. This Middle Way was actually a higher way. The Buddha took refuge from the howling of the eight winds in a state of complete equanimity and peace. He based his life on wisdom, compassion, and inner freedom.

### Ethics – A Port in the Storm

If we are to become truly free, we have to find a way to avoid being blown endlessly around by the worldly winds. As we have seen, the Buddha arrived at the final solution, seeing with deep wisdom that there is no fixed unchanging self. When this mirage of an 'I' with its ceaseless self-concern vanishes, its urgent demands for praise, pleasure, and so on die away. However, most of us are still a long way away from that radical transformation that stills the winds. What we need is a temporary shelter from them, a respite that will enable us gradually to explore life's true nature until we arrive at wisdom. The way in which the Buddha suggested we could shelter from the eight winds is by following his ethical recommendations, usually known in Buddhist tradition as precepts.

In looking at anything to do with Buddhist ethics, we need from the outset to strip away any assumptions that might be smuggled into the discussion from other spiritual traditions. Buddhism does not believe in a Creator God, and there is no question of our unethical actions giving offence to the Buddha, or any issue of divine retribution. A Buddha is by definition the embodiment of compassion, and will always have the welfare of all living beings at heart. Any suffering involved in not following the Buddhist precepts is entirely natural.

How can following these ethical precepts protect us from the eight winds and increase our freedom? Essentially, the precepts give us directions for acting ethically, in the same way that an Enlightened person will naturally act. Therefore by following the precepts we align our actions with those of someone who understands the nature of Reality. Our actions are then in harmony with how things really are, and their results are fulfilling. When we go against the precepts we act in ways which anyone who understood the true nature of things would never do. These actions are based on misunderstandings of life, such as the idea that we are a fixed self, ultimately separate from other living beings, so they quite naturally result in suffering.

The simplest and most common set of precepts in the Buddhist tradition is a set of five which, expressed in negative form, are: not to harm living beings, not to take what has not been given, not to engage in sexual misconduct, not to lie, and not to cloud the mind with intoxicants. Put positively, the ethical precepts involve making the effort to base our lives on love, generosity, tranquillity, truth, and awareness. Contacting these enduring, bedrock values gives us the strength to resist the blandishments of the pleasant winds and the threats of the unpleasant ones. These ethical precepts give us a different, and deeper, basis for deciding how to live and act than simply reacting to the forces of the eight winds.

### Freedom and the Fourth Precept

We could examine these five precepts at length, but as space is limited we shall take one precept as an example of how they work. We shall explore the precept of truthful speech, the one that could most obviously have rescued Crowhurst, and try to see how it can save us from suffering and expand our freedom.

With so much at stake for him, how could a precept of truthful speech have helped Crowhurst in practice? Clearly, it would not have been enough for him to have taken on the idea of speaking the truth as a kind of rule or commandment that he had to follow. That simplistic approach to morality is too brittle, and would have cracked under the strain of his situation. The precept would help someone in Crowhurst's position only if he had understood its fundamental significance for his life.

In the case of the fourth precept, the motivation to deceive ourselves or others naturally causes us suffering. We cannot gain true freedom if all the time we are distorting our world. If we are habitually untrue to ourselves, then our world – which we create with our words, our actions, and our thoughts – will be bent right out of shape. By doing this we distort others' perceptions as well, so they cannot let us out of the prison of untruth that we have created.

Crowhurst could have saved himself from his terrible predicament by one minute of openness. He said to his wife 'Are you all right at home? Are you sure you can cope with all the difficulties?' inviting her to rescue him by saying 'No, I'm not, do come back.' Tragically, but not surprisingly, she did not see what he was really asking her. Instead, all he had to do (it would have been agonisingly hard, he was in a terrible predicament, but there was still a way out) was say to his wife: 'I haven't sailed round the world. I didn't go round Cape Horn. My boat was in a bad way early on, so I faked my voyage.' That would have been terribly difficult to say, but had he done so he would have saved his life and sanity, and his children would still have had a father. It would have been deeply humiliating, but his life would have gone on. A new future would have opened up. Whether he went bankrupt or not, whether his marriage was saved, as a human being he would have gained a tremendous amount from that voyage – more than publicity, more than money, more than anything he could have bargained for.

Because Crowhurst had presented himself as someone who had gone round the world, when he asked his wife, in effect, to get him out of this mess, she did not understand what was going on. She thought he was concerned about her and the children, and gave him the exact opposite of what he wanted, which was an honourable way out, a decent excuse. If we have distorted our world we cannot expect other people to help us, because they are going to misinterpret our signals. It is up to us to remedy the situation, by returning to the truth, showing ourselves as we really are.

Because the precepts are based on the true nature of things, going against them tends to lead in the direction of disintegration. Donald Crowhurst, sadly, is an illustration of the extreme of this. He moves away from the fourth precept; he lets go of truth. He has his two logs and he jokes to his TV camera while hiding his own dark thoughts. As a result, he cracks into several pieces. Falsehood always tends to be disintegrating, psychologically and spiritually, and the truth is always integrating. In fact, truthfulness is the most powerful integrating factor for consciousness that there is. Buddhists tend to think of awareness, often referred to as mindfulness, as the fundamental integrating element in consciousness. But what is mindfulness? It is the awareness of the truth of your experience, moment by moment. When you are aware, you pay attention to what is there, without getting side-tracked into fantasy and illusion; you stay with the truth of what is happening in your body, your feelings, your mental states, and your environment.

Each of the five precepts, understood in its depth and fullness, can be virtually a path to freedom in itself. This is true in the case of the fourth precept. The thrust of this precept goes far beyond the avoidance of telling lies and the development of factual accuracy (important as they are). It invites us to embark on a voyage in search of the true nature of things. It means, if we really take it to heart, that everything we do should express the truth, should express reality as fully and deeply as possible. Of course, we can only speak the truth in the full sense if we think the truth; if we feel the truth; if we are trying to

live and breathe the truth. This feels very different from coldly
ticking off a checklist in our heads about whether we have been
factually accurate in our statements today.

All this relates very closely to freedom. On an everyday level,
practising seeing and describing things as they are gives our lives a
foundation of strength and certainty. We know more clearly who we
are and where we stand. Also, caring for the truth so that we hold to
it even under difficult circumstances enables us to withstand and
overcome limiting emotions such as fear and anxiety. Steering by a
compass pointing to the truth, we do not allow ourselves to be blown
off course by the worldly winds. Finally, the practice of seeking the
truth enables us to see the true nature of things and to liberate ourselves from the self-deception and fantasy that cause us suffering.

### Returning to the Truth

We have looked at the consequences of untruth, and the positive
vision that is implicit in the fourth precept. How are we to return to
the truth, to the extent that we have left it? In a way, it is drastically
simple. One of my Buddhist teachers was asked, 'What practice can
one do in order to develop openness?' His reply was, 'There isn't a
practice. You just open up.' That is all we have to do: take our courage
in both hands and show ourselves as we truly are.

This process of opening up is rendered much easier if we have
like-minded friends who empathize with our aspiration to become
freer, and whom we trust to have our best interests at heart. Nonetheless, however kind and sympathetic our friends may be, for them
to be able to help us we need, somewhere along the line, to show
ourselves. We shall have to take a leap and share with someone our
private log, the real one, and throw the false one overboard. If we
have wandered far from the truth, that will mean swallowing our
pride and climbing down from the unreal pedestal on which we have
been perching. But what a relief when it is done! It is only when you
show someone the log of your real journey, your true position, that
you discover how much energy was locked up in the tension between your appearance and your reality.

In case the prescription 'just open up' sounds too bald, we could
try following the method used by Ernest Hemingway. He said that
his way of writing while living in Paris was very simple. He would
sit down at his desk, try to find one true statement, and write it

down. Then another, and another. They did not have to be exalted or brilliant; they just had to be true. It is a powerful practice. Try doing it for half an hour: writing one true statement, then another, and another. Or even think or say a succession of true statements. Once you connect with the spirit of it, this becomes a practice of searching for truth, deeper and deeper.

If we work on finding true statements and persevere with this as a practice, then, among other positive consequences, we shall tend to trust other people with who we really are. This includes taking the risk of telling them how much we appreciate or love them – because we often hold back those truths too, as they feel risky. Thus – perhaps after some initial difficulty as they clear a backlog of distortion – when people seriously undertake this precept they often find their communication with other people is not only more truthful but also more affectionate.

Our exploration of this mariner's tale is nearly done. I have taken the fourth precept as an example to demonstrate the vital importance of ethics on the path to freedom. In doing so I have outlined an ideal, and it may take much work for us to approach it. Indeed, at times we may feel very far from it, unable or unwilling to give our true course and position in life. However, in Buddhism the precepts are seen as training principles. As with any training we may begin at a higher or a lower level, but wherever we start from what is important is that we keep making an effort. If we should fall into pessimism about our progress, we can comfort ourselves with the idea that the light of truth can never be extinguished. It may be obscured but it can always be found again. As we have seen, we can return to truth, we can return to the path towards freedom, by making 'one true statement'.

To put it poetically, it is as if there is a core of truth deep within our being. However far away from it we stray, we still somehow feel – on some subterranean level – a pressure for the reality of things to come out. Donald Crowhurst could have destroyed the records of his deception. He could have thrown away his original log. Had he done so he would have left us with a new *Mary Celeste* mystery – an empty boat sailing along in good order with no indication of what happened to its occupant. It may be that by the end he was too mentally unhinged to destroy the evidence. However, I prefer to think that in his final moments Donald Crowhurst was truthful – that he wanted to communicate what had really happened. So he left those two logs behind him as a trail to the truth, so that the whole story could be pieced together. He left us a final message, a warning, not to sail on the seas of untruth, not to allow the worldly winds to determine our course. I am very grateful to him for his honesty.

# PART TWO

Early Buddhism

2

# A Quest in the Houses of the Dead

*A Cure for Death?*

In this chapter we shall be looking at a very well-known incident
from the time of the Buddha. The tale is so frequently told that you
might wonder, when the Buddhist tradition is so rich, why we
should turn to it again. However, certain incidents are recounted
frequently because they have much to teach us about the path to
freedom. These stories are wells of inspiration that never dry up.

The story comes from the *Therīgāthā*, a collection of songs and
stories of some of the Buddha's Enlightened female disciples. It is a
very important collection indeed. Apart from being inspiring in
itself, it provides 'the earliest extant evidence of women's experience
in any of the world's religious traditions'.[3] In these stories we hear
the testimony of the first women in recorded history to break
through into the freedom of Enlightenment. Though they lived 2,500
years ago and dwelt in obscurity as wanderers, meditating at the foot
of trees and wearing robes of cast-off rags, yet, almost miraculously,
their names, their stories, and their songs of freedom have come
down to us. For 500 years the stories of women such as Subhā and
Paṭācārā were passed down orally, until finally they were written on
palm-leaf manuscripts, which themselves would have required fre-
quent painstaking recopying.

It is in this way that the name of a woman who was derided as 'the
daughter of a nobody' came to be known to millions of Buddhists
today. Her name is Kisā Gotamī. She was born to poor parents, and
she herself was frail and thin. ('Kisā' means 'lean, haggard,

emaciated' in Pāli.) However, when she grew to marriageable age, which is quite young in India, she managed to find a husband from a prosperous family. As with many brides, though, the transition to her husband's house was very hard. Her life was made miserable by members of her husband's family, who looked down on her for being 'the daughter of a nobody' – which in India is even worse than being a nobody's son.

After some time Gotamī did the one thing that could raise her status in the eyes of her in-laws. She was so frail and thin that perhaps her husband's family had been doubtful if she could bear children. If so, she proved them wrong. She bore her husband a son. As the triumphant producer of a male offspring, she could bask in a position of new respect within her family, and with her neighbours in the city of Sāvatthi where she lived. She had been a nobody's daughter, and now she was the mother of a somebody.

For a while, Gotamī lived happily in the centre of her family. But suddenly and unexpectedly her life foundered. Her husband died. He had certainly loved her – there could be no other reason for him to have chosen the daughter of such a poor family as a bride.[4] Now he was gone, and Gotamī found herself surrounded by people who did not care for her at all. With her marriage sunk without trace, she clung to the spar of being the mother of a male heir. She watched over her young son proudly, as he learned to walk and began to range further in his games.

You can imagine that for a young widow, surrounded by an uncaring household, seeing her dead husband's features reflected in his small offspring, gaining respect only for being a mother, her young child became her lifeline to happiness, even her reason for existing. So when, a little while later, the child became seriously ill, Gotamī was beside herself with worry. She had been called Kisā Gotamī before she married. Now, sitting at the bedside, not eating, she grew thinner yet. Her loss in weight paralleled that of her two-year-old, who could afford to lose it even less than she. He wasted away in front of her. Before she could begin to believe it, her son was dead.

Gotamī's mind was overwhelmed by the tragedy. She simply couldn't accept that her child had died. Fighting to deny the truth, she became submerged in a madness of grief. She picked up the dead child and, to the despair of her relatives, carried the bundle on her hip out of the house as if he were still alive. She began going from house to house, saying her son was sick and needed medicine. At each house the initial sympathetic response turned to revulsion when a glance into the bundle she carried was enough to pronounce it a corpse. They turned from the vacant eyes of the child to the crazed eyes of the mother and said 'Medicine! What's the use?'

Still Gotamī fought to drown out the impatient messages, struggling from one house to the next. She found little sympathy. After all, she might be carrying infection on her hip around the city. Eventually someone did take pity on her, and gently suggested that she take her child to see the Buddha, who was staying outside the city, and ask him for medicine. It was the only constructive suggestion, the only hope she had been offered. So the slight figure with her limp burden struggled along the track out of Sāvatthi to the place where the Enlightened One was teaching.

The Buddha's quiet eyes looked into the tear-streaked face of Gotamī, summing up the situation as she beseeched him for medicine for her child. Those who had been listening to his teaching waited, intrigued to see how the Buddha would deal with this madwoman. To their surprise, he agreed to her request. Gotamī's face lit up. Her child was sick and desperately needed medicine, and nobody in Sāvatthi had understood or been prepared to help. Now at last someone had responded in her hour of need; she had found an Enlightened teacher who would cure her child.

The onlookers shifted uneasily. The Buddha was renowned as a teacher who held unwaveringly to the truth. What was the point of colluding with the fantasies of this pathetic young girl? The Buddha was telling the poor little thing to go into Sāvatthi and bring back an ingredient for the medicine. What could bring the dead back to life? What he was asking for wasn't even unusual. It was mustard, the most common condiment of all. People ate it every day, but it didn't prevent them dying.

Gotamī's eyes lit up. She could picture the container of mustard seed in the kitchen of her own house. She would hurry home. But then the Buddha added one condition. The mustard seed had to come, he said, from a house in which nobody had died. Gotamī frowned for a moment, as her dead husband came to mind. She could not go home. But everyone had mustard seed; she would go into the outskirts of Sāvatthi and ask at the first house she came to.

She paid hurried, grateful respects to the Buddha, and set off towards the city as fast as the bundle on her hip would allow.

Gotamī's heart was pounding as she hurried along the road back to Sāvatthi. She reached a small village, full of old houses, and called at the first. The old woman she spoke to was wary of her at first, but when all she wanted was a little mustard seed, she was happy to oblige. As the two women went into the kitchen Gotamī asked if anyone had died in the house. The old woman's face changed. It was hard to be reminded of so much grief. Her family had lived in the house for generations. She told Gotamī of just some of the deaths that had occurred in her long lifetime.

Gotamī didn't take the list in. She was wasting time here, as this old woman spoke of parents and grandparents, brothers and sisters. She made her excuses and hurried on to the next house. Here she met another woman, as the men were mainly working in the fields, younger this time, maybe five or six years older than herself. The same willingness to spare a little mustard, but then the change of expression, and a wry 'Don't remind me!' in response to her second question. This woman had lost her father-in-law two years ago, and then there were the two stillborn babies....

What bad luck, that both houses she had tried had been touched by death. Gotamī pushed on, thinking only of her sick son, and of returning as quickly as possible to the calm man in the forest who could cure him. Several houses later she still had no mustard seed, and was beginning to realize that her task would not be as easy as she had at first thought. Five houses further on, her pace had slowed, and she was taking in more of the accounts of death that everyone told her. It was dawning on her that what had happened to her was not a unique stroke of bad luck. Everywhere she tried, people had their own stories of accidents and illness. A phrase someone had used to her went round in her head: 'The living are few compared to the dead.'

There were only a couple more houses left in the village, and Gotamī dreaded trying them, knowing what she would hear. Imperceptibly her hopes of finding the mustard seed had drifted away, and the stories of loved ones who had died became her main interest. When she emerged from the last house, the road into Sāvatthi lay before her. However, she turned away, saying to herself, 'This is how things will be in the whole town. The Buddha knew that, and out of care for me sent me on this quest.' Then, following the directions she had asked for in the last house, she calmly walked along a track across some fields.

Eventually she came to the village charnel ground. There she lay down the bundle she had carried so far, and which had become so heavy. She was still racked with grief, but she was sane once again. Indeed, she was far wiser and more mature than the previous day. In her crisis, through the Buddha's kindness she had been brought up against the nature of life, death, and humanity. As she laid down the son she knew was dead, she sang a verse expressing what she had realized:

*No village law is this, no city law,*
*No law for this clan, or for that alone,*
*For the whole world – and even for the gods in heaven,*
*This is the truth: Everything is impermanent!*[5]

Then, very tired, but much lighter without her burden, she went back to the Buddha. His calm eyes took in the change in her in a moment, but he still asked if she had brought the mustard seed. There was no need to explain to him. She replied simply: 'The little mustard seed has done its work.' Then she asked him formally to accept her as a disciple, and to allow her to become one of his wandering followers. In this moment when she was completely open to him, the Buddha reached into her heart and plucked out the root of her grief and suffering. Speaking quite simply, he emphasized that if your heart is centred on children and possessions, and you cling to them in your thoughts, then when death comes, as it must, you will be unprepared. You will be swept away by it, like a sleeping village struck by a flood in the night.

These words shook Gotamī's frail frame to its core. Then they expanded outwards in a burning sphere of understanding. In a few moments she relived her recent life and crazed grief; the villagers' stories rang in her ears once again; in her mind's eye the great city of Sāvatthi was filled with houses of the dead; the whole sleeping world was swept away. It was true, everywhere and always: everything was impermanent. Everything she saw mirrored it; everything she heard echoed it. She knew it in her heart; she would never deny it or forget it. This understanding caused a chain reaction of realizations in Gotamī. As one by one her illusions about life fell away, she saw what transcends death. Suddenly she understood the nature of her own mind, and the sun of freedom dawned in her heart.

### The Noble Quest

The image of the thin figure of Kisā Gotamī walking from house to house, encumbered with the weight of the lifeless child on her hip, denying the truth, is one which can stand as a symbol for much of the human condition. For the rest of this chapter we shall be reflecting on different aspects of her story, as she gradually transforms herself through the catalysing teaching of the Buddha.

Gotamī's story divides broadly into two stages. There is her early quest for happiness through marriage and children; then there is her quest for Enlightenment. The contrasting nature of these two searches is spelled out in a Pāli *sutta* in which the Buddha talks about his own life.[6] As we saw in the last chapter, he had been the son of an important public figure, and had married and had a child before deciding to give up everything to search for the truth of existence. The Buddha describes this turnaround in his life in terms of moving from the 'ignoble quest' (Pāli, *anariya pariyesana*) to the 'noble quest' (*ariya pariyesana*). *Pariyesana* means a 'search, quest, or inquiry'; *anariya* means 'ignoble, undignified, low, common, or uncultured'; *ariya* means 'noble, distinguished, right, good, or ideal'.

The ignoble quest, according to the Buddha, is that – being yourself subject to impermanence, to old age, sickness, and death – you go in search of, or quest after, that which is also impermanent and liable to suffering. It is as if you are in danger of drowning, and in trying to save yourself you cling to someone else who is also sinking below the waves.

What is the alternative? The noble quest or search is one in which someone who is liable to impermanence and suffering realizes the danger of such things and, in the Buddha's words, seeks 'what is unborn, ageless, disease-free, immortal, unsorrowing, and incorruptible – the matchless haven from bondage, that is Nibbāna, Enlightenment.' It is as if you were drowning but then clutched a lifeline that pulled you to dry land, into a different element or dimension altogether.

In this sutta the Buddha explains that it was his realization that there were these two quests open to a human being that caused him to go forth from home, to strive and struggle as a homeless wanderer, a homeless spiritual warrior. This quest was fulfilled when he gained the insight into the nature of Reality that freed him from the shackles of birth and death. At that point he exclaimed, 'Open are the doors of the deathless.'

The whole of this book is about that noble quest, because that is the search for true freedom. However, the quest will not necessarily entail literally leaving behind worldly involvements. The noble quest is never a running away from genuine responsibility. Many of us have partners and children, ageing parents, or others who rely on us. We cannot simply ditch them and head for some mountain retreat – even if we ourselves were capable of making good use of such a situation.

What then of Siddhārtha, who was to become the Buddha? Did he not shirk responsibility? If we were to transpose his story to modern Britain wouldn't it sound rather familiar: a young man doing a 'midnight flit', leaving his wife and child and disappearing off to hide in the country somewhere, beyond the clutches of the Child Support Agency? We could argue that he was fortunate, as the son of a ruler, knowing that his wife Yasodharā and his son Rāhula would be well provided for by his wealthy family. (Marriage in India at that time was usually not so much the romantic person-to-person bond that we tend to imagine, but more of a pragmatic family alliance.) Doubtless that was an important consideration in his mind. However, Siddhārtha took responsibility in a way that seems almost unimaginable. He became intensely aware of the existential situation that he – and all those he loved and cared for – were in. He could visualize his father, wife, son, and relatives growing old, growing sick, and dying.

We are all in his position but, not seeing any solution, we usually keep this awareness at the back of our minds, burying our heads firmly in the sand. Siddhārtha, however, felt the pain of his situation so intensely – and also had an intuition that there was a cure for the existential ills that he and his family faced – that he took responsibility by leaving. If he had been a father whose family were starving, no one would have questioned it when he went off to forage for food to put an end to their suffering. Similarly, seeing his loved ones starved of understanding of the nature of life, and bound to suffer as a result, Siddhārtha went foraging for freedom.

### Clutching our Bundles

Whether or not we make drastic changes to our outer circumstances, following the path to freedom does involve a radical reorientation of our being. We need first to examine our situation honestly and sincerely. Being ourselves subject to change and suffering, can we hope to be free when we are seeking satisfaction from people and situations which are themselves impermanent and liable to suffering? Unfortunately, we can have no certainty from our experience that there is a 'deathless state' of total happiness and freedom. All we usually have to rely on is the testimony of people like the Buddha, and sometimes a vague intuition of something deep within our being. The noble quest will not be easy. The odds that it will turn out well may not seem very high. But what is the alternative? Wringing any real security or lasting happiness from the ignoble quest is simply impossible. We need to keep reflecting on this until we arrive at a definite conclusion – a decision that moves us to action.

Why do we cling so to the ignoble quest? I'm afraid the Buddhist answer is not very flattering. Watching Gotamī wandering the streets of Sāvatthi with the bundle on her hip, crazily seeking medicine for a dead child, we may have shaken our heads, or felt a little superior to her. But, according to the Buddha, all those who have not gained some degree of Enlightenment, all 'worldlings' (Pāli, *puthujjanas*) are crazy. We are all mad – from the Enlightened point of view – because we believe in what are called 'upside-down views' (Pāli, *viparyāsas*). We treat the impermanent as if it was permanent; the unsatisfactory as if it could give us lasting satisfaction; the ever-changing process of life as if it were composed of fixed, separate entities.

We may not believe these ideas rationally, in the sense that if questioned we can acknowledge that we shall one day die, or that it's unreasonable to expect money, a job, or a sexual relationship to give us total satisfaction. Yet if we look at how we live our lives, we shall see that we very often act as if we believe these ideas. We are taken by surprise by the grey hairs, the decreasing energy, the accelerating birthdays. We stake our happiness on a sexual relationship. We sacrifice health to accumulate wealth, then spend our hard-earned gains on trying to stave off illness. In particular we think we have a fixed unchanging self, when in reality (as we shall see more and more clearly in later chapters) 'me' is a fixed concept slapped on the shifting sands of our mental and physical processes.

It is because we believe these topsy-turvy views that we tend to follow the ignoble quest. So we are none of us entirely sane, and we should not feel too superior to Gotamī, clinging to her dead son. We all struggle along carrying a dead weight, clutching a bundle, of views, ideas, and opinions that we cannot put down. Gotamī's bundle, her dead child, is both her past happiness and her future hopes – for her son was the guarantor of her future status, as well as the future joy on which she centred her life. We too carry round the past: old hurts and resentments which we won't put down. We also drag along our hopes and fears for the future, for craving springs eternal, along with hope. As we get older, the circle of realistic possibilities for what we might do with our lives narrows like a noose, until we are carrying round a bundle of 'might have beens' and 'if onlys'. These burdens prevent us from living in the present moment, encountering ourselves and life directly, here and now, which would be our salvation.

All too often, this is the human condition, and when we recognize it we begin to look for medicine, for a cure. So Gotamī, with her bundle, goes from house to house, door to door. But most people don't respond; some are even rude and unkind to her. They are confronted by their own impotence in the face of death, their help-lessness as followers of the ignoble quest, and so they draw back. They distance themselves from Gotamī, telling themselves that she is crazy.

At last she finds someone who understands, who can empathize with her plight. This person perhaps sees that we are all carrying the bundle of the question of death on our hips. They recognize that her question is really an existential one, about the human condition. So they direct her to the Buddha, who after much striving has found answers to the deepest questions of humanity.

The Buddha only needs one look at Gotamī, as she trails into his presence, to know that there is no point in giving her lectures on impermanence. You cannot give anyone your spiritual experience; you can only set up conditions whereby they will gain their own. Thus he sends her on another search, on a further round of the doors of Sāvatthi. This stratagem is often quoted as an example of the Buddha's 'skilful means' (Pāli, *upaya*) – the shrewd and subtle ways in which an Enlightened person, motivated by deep compassion, helps people to find their freedom.

### Searching for the Mustard Seed

The task the Buddha sets Gotamī seems a simple one. Mustard was probably the most common spice in India at that time.[7] Yet there is one condition – the seed must not be tainted with death. During her search Gotamī soon discovers that death is as common as mustard seed. That is still true today – just less obvious. If you were to go around your locality asking for sugar from a house where nobody had died, the task would probably not be too difficult. Nowadays people live longer, and tend to die in hospitals and hospices. We have removed death from our bedrooms and tidied it away. We have managed to hold it at bay, using medical science, for a few more decades. However, it is still there, as common as sugar.

In fact, death is becoming increasingly common. The world's population is growing; accelerating past 6,000,000,000 human beings. We naturally tend to talk of an increasing birth rate: of more people coming into the world, more mouths to feed. Yet every one of those births will result in a corresponding death. The larger the world's population, the more people are sitting in Death's waiting-room.

You may be thinking I am labouring the point, and this chapter is becoming depressing. Certainly, if there were no alternative to the ignoble quest there would be no point in looking at life. But once we become convinced that there is a path to freedom, then looking life square in the eye can only help us. Seeing the dangerous situation we are in will then motivate us to put more effort into following the noble quest. In any case, a head-down ostrich is a very defenceless creature indeed.

### Gotamī's Return to the Buddha

Eventually, as she drags the dead weight on her hip from house to house, Gotamī manages to hear other people's experience. She feels for them, and that fellow feeling leads her out of her hell of grief and self-pity. She lays down her bundle, expresses her new-found understanding that everything is impermanent, and returns to the Buddha, telling him that the little mustard seed has done its work. The Buddha's medicine has cured her of her illusions about life. She is then left with only one option, one desire: to follow the noble quest. So she commits herself to putting the quest for freedom at the centre of her life, relying on the Buddha's teaching and his Enlightened followers to assist her in achieving that goal.

To use the traditional phrase, she goes for Refuge to the Buddha, Dharma, and Sangha – often called the Three Jewels of Buddhism. Seeing that mundane life is treacherous, beguiling, and unfulfilling, she pledges herself to gain Enlightenment as the Buddha has done, to follow his teaching, the Dharma, as the path, and to participate in the Sangha, the spiritual community he founded, particularly relying on his advanced disciples. Going for Refuge is sometimes seen merely as the gateway to the path to freedom, a formal way of becoming a Buddhist. In reality, it is a repeated process, a deepening commitment that is repeated again and again. You could even say that Going for Refuge *is* the path to freedom.

So deeply has Gotamī seen through the fantasies and illusions of everyday life that no sooner has she first gone for Refuge than she becomes an advanced disciple herself. This breakthrough is triggered by the Buddha's very direct and personal teaching to her:

> *To those whose heart on children and on goods*
> *Is centred, clinging to them in their thoughts,*
> *Death comes like a great flood in the night,*
> *Bearing away the village in its sleep.*

Through this catalyst, she gains a direct, intuitive realization of the truth, and becomes a 'Stream-entrant'. Stream-entry is a decisive point on the path to freedom. With the attainment of this degree of realization, you experience the fruits of the noble quest so strongly that you can never lose them. You know for yourself that the Buddha's teaching is true, that there is a state of fulfilment and true security beyond suffering. Having experienced it you can no longer fall back to following the ignoble quest. You still have old habitual forces in your mind that may pull you off the path from time to time, but the balance has decisively shifted, your continued progress towards freedom is assured.

### Being Nobody and Somebody

One of the major themes of Gotamī's story is that of her changes in status. She is born into a poor family, and is despised until she marries a husband from a much wealthier background, at which point Gotamī's status in her own family would have risen. However, in her new surroundings she is again looked down upon for her humble origins. Then her position changes once more when she gives birth to a son. For a while she can bask in her new role as a mother, until she is cast down once more. It is clear from the text that she is not only distraught over her son's death, she is also aware that her status is thus reduced. She faces a bleak future as a childless widow, in a household in which she has been valued only for being a mother. One of the reasons she denies her son's death is that she is clinging desperately to her position. Finally, having acknowledged the true state of things, she gives up all thoughts of status, and becomes simply a homeless wanderer, begging her food, wearing only a plain robe made of rags. Even in that situation there were gradations, and she eventually became renowned for her asceticism – for being prepared to wear robes of exceptionally coarse material – though by that time she was completely unconcerned about praise or blame, renown or obscurity.

These changes in status are common to all of us. At different stages of our lives, or as we embark on new projects, others' views of us change, and our own perception of our value fluctuates. Often we take this process for granted, but we can learn much from exploring it. If we do so we shall see that the value that we place on ourselves is always relative to something else: we feel high or low compared to other people, or in comparison with our past position or our future prospects. We also begin to see that high and low status are related to each another. Through this kind of reflection we come to understand that status or position is not an absolute, or a given part of situations. Rather, it is a mental construct, and one which we can step out of, leaving ourselves much freer.

When people embark on the Buddhist path they often become confused about the whole issue of status and ego. They gather that Buddhism regards egotism as the source of our suffering. They also learn that Buddhism teaches *anattā* – that there is no fixed self or ego. Thus they often end up making great efforts not to display any signs of ego, whilst at the same time contriving to believe that the ego doesn't exist. Needless to say this confusion causes strain and tension.

Much of the problem comes from misunderstanding the doctrine of *anattā*. This does not say that 'you don't exist' – it does not deny the existence of a relative, contingent self or ego. In line with the fundamental Buddhist understanding that all phenomena are impermanent, it denies that the ego or self is a fixed, unchanging entity. Thus although this is not the traditional explanation, it might be helpful to see *anattā* as the doctrine that we are giving birth to a new self in every moment. However we approach it, understanding *anattā* should be a very positive realization, because it means there is absolutely nothing about us that cannot undergo endless positive transformation.

It may help to sort out these difficulties if we distinguish between three broad levels of human development. Firstly, there is a level on which someone has not established much individuality in the positive sense. They are not very self-aware. They usually go along with the eight worldly winds, and as a result are largely conditioned by the environments and social groups in which they find themselves. The second level is one of greater self-awareness. On this level one thinks and feels for oneself, forging a stronger individuality, and becoming less negatively affected by the environment. Thirdly, there is the level on which one develops insight into the true nature of things. On this level you begin to transcend the distinction between yourself as limited subject and the world viewed as inherently-existing things and people. Thus one moves from a weak sense of self, easily overwhelmed by situations and group pressures, to a positive sense of self in which one lives with greater awareness, and this awareness allows one to make more individual choices. Finally, one dismantles the idea of being a fixed self, however positive.

Thus we progress from being nobody very much to being somebody in a very positive human way, and finally we transcend even that state, and become 'nobody' once again – in the sense of an identity so broad that it can no longer be defined. This last stage is embarked upon at Stream-entry, when you know with certainty that there is no fixed unchanging you to die or to worry about. So Gotamī, who had been a 'nobody's daughter' and had then relied on her child in order to become somebody, discovered through deep awareness that there was a profound way of being nobody. The barrier of her fixed ideas about herself was decisively broken, and a blissful flow of creative energy poured through her, a spontaneous up-welling of happiness and understanding.

These distinctions should allow us to clarify the difficulties that arise when people confuse the first and third of these stages. Someone may have powerful or unusual experiences in the first stage, in which their ego-identity is overwhelmed and submerged, and may mistake these for spiritual experiences of the third stage. Or someone with a low sense of self-esteem, who is dominated by the people with whom they come into contact, may wrongly believe they are displaying the spiritual quality of lack of ego.

Let's end this section by looking a little more at the question of self-esteem. These days much pop psychology is devoted to trying to help us feel okay about ourselves. This will only work if we are encouraged to develop self-esteem based on what is genuinely positive in our lives. Whilst it is true that many of us suffer from irrational self-hatred and lack of self-esteem, it is no good trying to give people a positive sense of themselves regardless of how they are acting. One can certainly develop a certain amount of psychological confidence through mundane success; however, true self-esteem comes from a sense that we are living a life that is valuable for ourselves and others. When we set out on the path to freedom we have a sense that our life is meaningful. We feel on good terms with ourselves because we are working to make our lives an expression of our ideals, which means practising ethical values such as generosity and concern for others' welfare. Out of these qualities a sense of genuine and sustainable self-esteem naturally develops.

### Doors to Death and to the Deathless

In 1990 I was working to finish my book *Meeting the Buddhas* and needed some part-time work to keep myself afloat financially, so I took a job as a door-to-door fund-raiser for the environmental charity Friends of the Earth. It was demanding but fascinating work. It was demanding because I would have to ring many doorbells, and receive many rejections and disappointments, for each new supporter that I found. It was fascinating to see the very different worlds behind the doors. In the course of a couple of hours' door knocking I would enter worlds that angered or saddened me, worlds that felt like alien planets, worlds friendly and welcoming, and the occasional world that made me appreciate the human spirit.

Gotamī's search for a cure for death keeps taking her to the doors of houses around Sāvatthi. She too encounters rejection and disappointment, as well as sympathy and kindness. In her case this door-to-door search has a number of stages to it.

Firstly, there is her crazed quest for medicine after her son dies. This is a totally deluded search, born out of the tragedy of mundane life. Before we take up the spiritual life we may not be as crazed as Gotamī, but we are often in denial about the fact that life cannot be made permanently satisfactory, in denial that we and all those close to us will grow old, fall sick, and die. Occasionally that denial may take the form of naïve optimism, taking on trust what we might characterize as the advertising copywriters' view of life.

Secondly, there is Gotamī's search for mustard seed from a house in which no one has died. She is still searching in the wrong place, seeking the impossible. However, her situation has improved. She has met the Buddha, and taken his advice. Through his skilful means she is forced to engage with life in a deeper way, listening to people's stories. After we start practising the Dharma we shall still find that very often our old, unreconstructed, headstrong emotions will drag us away on the ignoble quest from time to time. It is all too easy to keep listening to the siren voices that tell us that something mundane will fix our lives. If only we had the mustard seed of a new house, a more loving partner, a better-paid job, surely we would live happily ever after.

But having heard the Dharma, we carry the teaching with us even as we are on the run from it. Sooner or later, if we have the courage to be honest with ourselves, we have to acknowledge that the teaching is right – our quest is futile. We are not going to find any mundane mustard seed that is not tainted with death. Then we make the journey back to the feet of the Buddha. We develop a deeper trust and confidence in his teaching, and go for Refuge more deeply to the Three Jewels. Human nature being what it is, this process of renewed hope in the ignoble quest, disillusionment, and return to the noble quest is likely to happen many times. Without making excuses for ourselves, it is sensible to expect it to happen. What is vitally important is that when we fall back into the ignoble quest we keep our eyes wide open so that we learn from the experience.

People who find it hard to accept their imperfections may easily develop a rather dissociated spiritual life. They desperately want to be the ideal person: a good Buddhist following the path to Enlightenment. Inevitably they are far from ideal, and they often feel irrational guilt at these backslidings. Then their failures to follow the Dharma may become furtive sorties on the ignoble quest; 'furtive' in the sense that they are not acknowledged to others, and are often not even fully conscious to themselves. This creates an unhealthy emotional split within the personality. (We are back to the theme of keeping two logs that we met with in the last chapter.)

Worse still, it means that such people learn nothing from their forays away from the noble quest. The bottom line is that whatever mirages of mundane life you follow, whatever pits of craving, jealousy, or pride you fall into, you should try to stay aware, wide awake to what is happening, and to see the true nature of the situation. Then, in a sense at least, you are still on the path to freedom, albeit on a meandering diversion. After all, mundane life isn't unfulfilling because the Buddha said so. It truly is unfulfilling in itself. At first, we may take what the Buddha says on trust, but our aim has to be to see for ourselves the truth of what he described. The Buddha taught from his own experience. We are just as surrounded by the experiences of life as he was. All we have to do is look at life, and at the workings of our own minds, deeply and clearly, and draw our own conclusions.

Gotamī's story seems only to describe two rounds of begging at doors, but implicit within it is a third. As one of the Buddha's homeless wandering followers, she would have spent the rest of her life begging for her food. Each day she would make a round of some houses near where she was staying, standing silent at their doors with her alms-bowl. This third round of standing at doors has a very different feeling from the wild grief of the previous two. Now she makes her round calm and aware, looking for nothing but enough food to sustain her, so that she can continue her life of meditation, reflection, and friendship. By this point her insight into Reality is burning ever brighter.

On her earlier crazed rounds she was hoping to find some physical cure for death and suffering. Now her expectations have changed. She does not burden people with impossible demands. From the doors of Sāvatthi she just hopes for a little rice and curry, regardless of whether anyone has died in the house. This is all she needs from these doors, because her own mind now provides her with all the fulfilment she could require. Like her teacher the Buddha, she has opened a door within her own mind, and stepped through it to experience the deathless. She is no longer looking to the mundane for a cure to birth and death. Her contentment and fulfilment come from within. She has only realistic and limited expectations of the mundane. Mustard seed is just mustard seed, one of the common ingredients in the curry and rice that is placed in her bowl.

To be truly happy and free we have to come to see the world through Gotamī's eyes. Chocolate is just chocolate; sex is just sex. A new car is just a shinier means of getting around, and the traffic queues are still there, just the same. These things are okay on their own level, but we can't expect them to make our lives fulfilling. Only the noble quest can do that. Only insight into the true nature of existence can finally fix our lives.

### A Big Lizard on an Ignoble Quest

Some years ago I was in Australia, staying with some friends in an isolated house in the bush outside Sydney. One afternoon there was a great commotion, with all the dogs barking, and the owners of the house ran outside to see what was happening. It turned out that a goanna had managed to find its way into the hen run. I had not seen one of these lizards before. It looked like a leftover from prehistoric times, about six feet long, with sharp claws. It was duly shooed away and the hens rescued.

Later I heard about a woman friend of mine who had once been chased by a goanna, and needed to show a good turn of foot to get away from it. I naturally assumed that goannas were aggressive to humans, but was told that this wasn't the case. In fact these lizards are frightened of us. Why, then, had the goanna chased her? It turned out that goannas' brains have not developed much since prehistoric times. To put it bluntly, they aren't very bright. I was told that when frightened their natural response is to climb up something, such as a tree, in order to get away. So when the goanna saw my friend and felt threatened, it naturally wanted to run up the nearest vertical object – which happened to be her. When she turned tail and fled, the dim creature started running after her, to climb up her, in order to get away from her! The person who told me this laughed about it, and said that what she should have done was lie down, whereupon the goanna would have just wandered off.

Apart from being a possibly useful piece of information if you are ever in the Australian bush, I am recounting this story because the goanna's behaviour (as interpreted for me by someone who, it has to be said, isn't a zoologist) is a perfect symbol for the ignoble quest.

Feeling threatened and insecure, it scurries along after the very object that is provoking its fear. Similarly we, afraid as we are of ageing, falling ill, and dying, can easily spend our whole life rooting around amongst impermanent phenomena, expecting them to give us security. No sooner does one fail us than our minds throw up another plan, another person, another palliative measure. We chase after mundane happiness and it outpaces us, but never by so much that we give up the pursuit. It is easy to keep on running, until our breathing stops.

There is an alternative to this endless futile chasing after mirages. Hopefully the image of Gotamī, who suffered so much, but who won her freedom, can inspire us to take up the noble quest. After her attainment of Stream-entry, Gotamī spent her time meditating in the forest in order to deepen the realization she had gained. (We know that one place where she meditated was called the Dark Wood.) As a result she made rapid progress. Finally her mind ripened to the point where she was on the verge of the full attainment of freedom. Again it was some words of the Buddha that caused her to break through, as she was looking at a flickering lamp:[8]

*The person who, living for a hundred years,*
*Never sees the path to the Deathless*
*Would be better living for a single day,*
*If they spent it seeing that path.*

Some time after she had attained that state of complete liberation, Gotamī recited some verses to the Buddha and his followers that encapsulated her understanding. You can hear the happiness and fulfilment ringing from them:

*I have developed the Noble Eightfold Path,*
*That goes to the state undying.*
*Enlightenment have I realized, and gazed*
*Into the mirror of the Dharma.*

*I, even I, am healed of my hurt,*
*Low is my burden laid, my task is done,*
*My heart is wholly set at liberty.*

There is something lovely about that 'I, even I'. Gotamī did not start out as some spiritual superwoman. She was a young grief-struck mother. Perhaps she was no more special than any of us. She just came to see clearly, with a little help from the Buddha, the need to follow the noble quest.

# 3

## Venturing Into the Forest

*A Full Moon Journey*

It is a beautiful night in ancient India. We are at the court of King Ajātasattu, in Rājagaha, the capital of the kingdom of Magadha. The King is sitting surrounded by his ministers on the upper terrace of his palace. It is October. The rainy season has passed; the night is cool. The finery of the King and his courtiers is lit by a full moon rising into the cloudless night sky. But the splendid appearance of the court bathed in the moonlight belies its reality, for the palace is a dark and unhappy place, full of intrigue and suspicion. Ajātasattu himself is deeply unhappy, racked with guilt. For many years he had longed to be King, while his father, Bimbisāra, lived to a robust old age. Finally, Ajātasattu became so frustrated that he plotted against his father. When Ajātasattu's treachery came to light, Bimbisāra was deeply shocked, but rather than punishing his son he agreed to step down and allow him to accede to the throne. However, Ajātasattu still felt uneasy, overshadowed by the image of the kind old king, who was much loved by his subjects. So he imprisoned his father, and finally allowed him to starve to death.

On beautiful nights like these the King experiences an uneasy mixture of emotions. The brilliant full moon seems to shine into dark recesses of his mind. It causes him to swing between hope that beauty and purity are still possible in the world, and a sense of his crime partially eclipsing the moon, preventing him from experiencing the peace and beauty of the scene. Out of this inner struggle comes the desire to visit a holy man who can help him to find some peace. He asks for suggestions: can someone recommend a sage with whom he could discuss spiritual matters? One by one his ministers propose six well-known teachers. But the King has seen them all before, and none of them has been able to bring him any peace. He has asked each the same question, and not one of them has been able to give him a satisfying answer.

Sitting in the moonlit assembly is a man called Jīvaka. His life has taken a strange path in order to bring him into the King's circle. He was born as the illegitimate son of Sālavatī, a courtesan in Rājagaha. Not wanting to be encumbered with a child, she had abandoned her new-born baby in a basket on a dust-heap. The baby was found there and a large crowd gathered. Prince Abhaya happened to be passing by, and seeing the crowd asked what the commotion was about. On hearing that an abandoned baby had been found, he enquired whether it was still alive. On being told that it was, he adopted it and brought the child up. The child was called Jīvaka. 'Jīva' means 'life', and the name sprang from the crowd crying 'It is alive!' As he grew older, Jīvaka was moved by the way he had been rescued and cared for, and decided to devote his life to helping others through the practice of medicine. He was very successful, and eventually became the King's personal physician.

Ajātasattu turns to his doctor, who has sat silent, and asks him if he has any suggestion to make. Jīvaka is a follower of the Buddha. Whenever the Buddha is staying near Rājagaha, Jīvaka goes to visit him twice a day. Indeed he has donated to the Buddha his own park near Rājagaha – known as the Ambavana, the Mango Grove. This park is more accessible than the Veḷuvana – the Bamboo Grove, the other main area used by the Buddha's wandering followers. Knowing that it is the practice of the Buddhist wanderers to meet together on the full moon night, Jīvaka suggests the King visit the Mango Grove to talk with the Buddha.

This is not a straightforward idea for the King. His father had been a great supporter of the Buddha – it was he who had donated the Bamboo Grove for the use of Buddhist wanderers. Also, years earlier Ajātasattu had been a supporter of Devadatta, one of the Buddha's followers who had become proud and competitive, and had tried to create a schism in the Buddhist community to his own advantage. However, Ajātasattu is suffering emotionally; the moon's serenity mocks him; he must try something to assuage the pain. He agrees to Jīvaka's suggestion.

For the King to make such a visit requires considerable preparation. He is too concerned for his safety and his position to travel with only a small group of attendants. So the royal elephants have to be led out and saddled, and the royal household made ready to travel. Finally a cavalcade leaves the palace, with no fewer than 500 elephants, with courtiers, the ladies of the royal household, attendants bearing torches, and, seated at the head of the procession on the state elephant, Ajātasattu, with Jīvaka in close attendance.

Most of the party start out in light-hearted mood, but as they travel out of the city and start coming closer to the Mango Grove, the King, who has spoken little, falls completely silent, and in response the chatter of those around him dies away. Ajātasattu has asked Jīvaka how many of the Buddha's followers will be gathered in the Mango Grove for their full moon meeting, and Jīvaka has told him there will be over a thousand people there. As the procession approaches the grove, the King begins to listen, with increasing unease, for some sound to indicate that a large meeting is taking place ahead of him.

Ajātasattu has had his own father put to death. He has made enemies in Kosala and other neighbouring states. He is not loved by his own subjects. He lives in a world of dark deeds and uneasy suspicions. As the elephants sway closer to the still silent Mango Grove, he begins to suspect the worst. The hairs on the back of his neck rise in fear, and he turns fretfully and threateningly to his guide: 'You are playing me no tricks, Jīvaka? You are not leading me into a trap and betraying me to my enemies?' Jīvaka tries to reassure him, but Ajātasattu's mind is not set at rest. He listens once more to the eerie silence coming from the Mango Grove, and then bursts out suspiciously, 'You said that the Buddha is meeting here with over a thousand of his followers. How can it be that there is no sound at all, not even a cough or a sneeze?'

His ministers could never have allayed the King's suspicions in such a situation. None of them could have prevented him from wheeling the state elephant back in the direction of the city and safety. However, Jīvaka is a physician, not a politician, and there is something about him that is credible and reassuring. He insists that he is not leading Ajātasattu into a trap, nor delivering him to his enemies. He urges him onwards, saying 'Go on, your majesty, straight on!' The King moves forward a little further, but uneasily. This brings him close enough to the grove for Jīvaka to point out a glow of light through the trees in the distance, which he says comes from lamps burning where the Buddha and his followers are meeting.

Somewhat reassured, the King urges his elephant down a small track that leads toward the light. After a while the track becomes too narrow for the beast to follow. The King dismounts, leaves his entourage of wives and servants, and walks forward through the trees with Jīvaka to guide him. Following the glow of the lights, they soon come upon a clearing. Here they see a great assembly of Buddhist wanderers, all sitting in meditation, silent and unmoving. Facing the assembly, his back to the pillar of a pavilion, sits the Buddha. He too is seated in meditation, his still figure emanating a thrilling silence that permeates the clearing with serenity, just as the moon bathes it with radiance.

The pair steal forward between the ranks of the meditators, and then the King, so used to striding about and issuing commands, stands respectfully and quietly near the Buddha. In that charmed circle of concentration and loving-kindness he finds himself at peace in a way he has not experienced since he took over the kingship. While he waits for the meditation to come to an end, he looks around at the serene gathering, and then whispers to Jīvaka, 'I wish that my son Udāyabhadda could know the same peace that there is in this assembly!'

The Buddha ends his meditation, slowly emerging from the deep pool of silence that has filled the grove. He greets Ajātasattu warmly, which is a relief as the King had not been sure what kind of reception he might receive given his past deeds. After they have exchanged polite enquiries, Ajātasattu feels that the time has come to ask his question. Much hangs on the answer. As we have seen, the King has put this same question to other spiritual teachers, including the six renowned teachers whom his courtiers had suggested he visit again tonight. He has never yet received a reply which satisfied him. The question is a simple one, down to earth and practical: 'Do your wandering followers gain tangible benefits from their way of life – as demonstrable as those gained by people who follow ordinary trades and professions?'

The Buddha smiles at the question, and replies at length. He starts with something very pragmatic and tangible indeed. He points out that if one of the King's slaves were to go forth as a homeless wanderer, whereas previously Ajātasattu would have ordered him around, he would now pay him respect. Others of his subjects would also improve their position in relation to the King by becoming wanderers.

The King wryly acknowledges that this is a clear benefit. However, his real interest lies in knowing if there are higher fruits of following the Buddha's path. In response the Buddha outlines step by step all the stages of the path to Enlightenment. He begins by describing how people listen to his teaching, and having developed confidence in it decide to go forth as homeless wanderers. Then through living ethically by following the precepts (as we saw in Chapter 1) they begin to experience calm, relaxation, and confidence. In addition they practise awareness of the senses, and contentment with a simple life. With this foundation they are able to overcome the five hindrances that prevent entry into higher states of consciousness: desire for sense-experience, ill will, sloth and torpor, restlessness and anxiety, and doubt. The Buddha likens the feelings of a wanderer who has overcome these hindrances to those of someone who has been freed from debt, from prison, or from slavery.

The King is already impressed, but the Buddha continues still further. He evokes, with beautiful images, the various stages of deep meditative concentration known as *jhāna* which his followers experience when they have overcome the hindrances – each one more subtle, refined, and deeply fulfilling than the last. For the tortured Ajātasattu these evocations of deepening happiness and serenity are like descriptions of beautiful lakes and streams to someone dying of thirst.

The Buddha does not stop even there. He describes how the wanderer can then, using the powerfully focused states of mind produced by these meditations, investigate the body and mind and come to a decisive understanding of their true nature. At each stage the Buddha points out to the King how what he has described is a tangible benefit that can be experienced, and how it is 'higher and sweeter than the last'.

Even now the Buddha has not finished leading the King imaginatively up the rainbow way of development to which his teaching gives access. Next he describes how the wanderer's mind can become so concentrated and purified that they experience super-normal powers such as clairaudience and telepathy, knowledge of their own and others' past existences, and deep intuitive insight into the law of karma – the consequences of people's volitional actions.

Finally, the Buddha portrays for his royal visitor how the wanderer arrives at total understanding of the Four Noble Truths, and knows decisively that his or her ignorance of the true nature of life and consciousness has been destroyed, and that all the restless yearnings caused by that ignorance have been stilled. The wanderer then recognizes that he or she has accomplished the whole path to freedom. They are completely liberated from suffering, and its causes have finally vanished.

The King is deeply moved by the Buddha's description – so much so that he goes for Refuge, and pledges himself to follow the path which the Buddha has brought so vividly to life for him in imagination. Not only that. He is so affected that he confesses the awful crime of killing his father, who had been a good and just man. The Buddha accepts this revelation without shock. He simply comments that to acknowledge one's faults for what they are helps prevent falling into them in the future.

Ajātasattu is pleased and delighted by all that has happened. He feels lighter and freer than he has for many years, but the effects of his terrible crime still have an obscuring effect on his mind. At this point, when he could have entered into even deeper communication with the Buddha, his old cares begin to tug at him once more. He remembers all the people waiting for him outside the charmed circle of the grove. Old cares and concerns begin to insinuate themselves into his mind. Excusing himself by saying that he has affairs of state to attend to, he takes his leave of the Buddha. Then, with Jīvaka once more at his side, he follows the track back through the trees to his waiting courtiers and elephants. Soon the noisy procession can be heard moving away in the direction of the city.

In the stillness of the clearing, the Buddha is discussing his meeting with Ajātasattu with those around him. He is pleased that the King was moved by his teaching. However, he also expresses regret that their communication could not have gone even deeper. The Buddha says, with great sadness in his voice, that had it not been for the terrible crime which weighed so much on his mind, Ajātasattu could have gained Stream-entry that very night.[9]

*Leaving Home for the Forest*

In this story we have 'ventured into the forest' to meet the Buddha, and some of his wandering followers. How did the Buddha live, who were these 'wanderers' who followed him, and what can we learn from them about our own quest for freedom? According to tradition, the Buddha left home when he was 29 (though in some Buddhist texts one gains the impression of someone younger). As we have seen, after six years of practising the most dreadful austerities, he finally discovered the Middle Way between the indulgence in pleasure he had known during his life at home, and the asceticism which he took to the limits of survival in his search for freedom.

In leaving behind his wife and family, the Buddha was following a trend that was very common in northern India at that time. From about a hundred years before, a whole movement had grown up of people leaving domestic responsibilities and going from place to place, begging their food, in a search for truth and freedom. The area was very prosperous at the time, and could support this large population of non-productive wanderers. These seekers after truth were often held in high esteem by ordinary people.

We do not really know what caused this movement in society. India at this time was seeing the development of city-states, but that does not account for the phenomenon. People who became wanderers are often represented as saying that they found their life at home cramped and limiting. It is clear that, whatever it was that led them to do it, leaving home was for most of them the beginning of a quest for freedom. Naturally there were a number of philosophers and yogic practitioners who claimed to be able to show people the path to truth and liberation. As we have seen, six of the most famous of these were suggested to the King by his ministers, but the King had visited them all before, and their answers had left him unsatisfied.

Although later Buddhist texts portray the Buddha as a monk, the head of an order of monks and nuns who lived by a carefully prescribed code of discipline, this is almost certainly a later reinterpretation of the Buddha's life. The Buddha undoubtedly left home in search of freedom. He lived the life of a homeless wanderer, and gained Enlightenment through meditation. After that he would have continued to spend time in the forest, occupied mainly with meditation, as well as venturing out to centres of population to teach. He gathered around him people of many lifestyles, both wanderers and house-dwellers, who followed his teaching of the way to liberation.

It is clear that people who stayed in their domestic situations were able to gain Enlightenment by practising the various aspects of the path that the Buddha outlined to Ajātasattu. However, the paradigm for following the path to freedom was to step outside conventional society and go into the *araṇya*. This Sanskrit word literally means 'forest', but it connotes the wilderness, the 'no man's land' where you are on your own, under nobody's jurisdiction. The *araṇya* could be the forest or jungle, the mountains or the desert, or a place that people usually avoid – such as a cremation ground or somewhere reputed to be haunted.

At that time most of northern India was covered in thick forest, and although there were a few great cities, such as Sāvatthi, most people lived in villages. It would only require a few minutes' walk into the forest to leave behind everyone you knew and your entire life so far. The forest was relatively undistracting, and provided the best conditions for meditation. It allowed a deep contact with nature and wildlife and therefore with death and the understanding of impermanence. The forest lifestyle was simple and peaceful. Of course there were hardships. Those who followed the wandering life had to come to terms with snakes, wild beasts, and stinging insects, as well as the uncertainty of what – if anything – would be placed in their begging-bowls. But still, compared to the situations they had left behind, they lived largely without mundane concerns.

One of the early Buddhist wanderers called Bhaddiya, who had been a king, was overheard by his fellows sitting in the forest saying aloud to himself, 'Oh, it's bliss!' Those who overheard him thought that he was wasting his time reminiscing about his life as a king. But it transpired that when he was a king he had never felt safe, and had been surrounded by armed guards day and night. Compared to that, it was his simple peaceful life in the forest that was bliss.[10]

### The Forest as Symbol

We have seen what the forest meant to the early wanderers who often lived within it. In this section we shall look at the forest as a symbol, and read Ajātasattu's story in that light. In the rest of this chapter we shall use both the literal and symbolic meanings of our story to see what we can learn from it.

On a symbolic level, leaving home and going into the forest symbolizes leaving the hurly-burly of the everyday mind and its concerns, and venturing into the depths of consciousness. In the inner forest one's mind is simple and peaceful. This inner journey also symbolizes leaving behind any persona – the social mask we employ to smooth our relations with other people.

Thus we can see Ajātasattu's night-time journey in both literal and symbolic terms. Literally, he leaves his palace and goes out of the city to meet a holy man. The meeting impresses him deeply and frees him enough – at least temporarily – to enable him to recognize the path to freedom and to confess his crime. Symbolically, he leaves behind his surface level of consciousness with all its concerns. He moves beyond defining himself by his position. He lets go of the elephants and courtiers and other trappings that reinforce his egotistical sense of being King. As he walks into the forest, like Lear on the heath, he becomes just another human being.

The Zen Buddhist teacher Keichū once received a visitor, who announced his arrival by sending in his calling card. It read 'Kitagaki, Governor of Kyoto'. Far from being flattered that such an important person had come to see him, Keichū told his attendant to send him away. The Governor was stunned to receive such a rebuff. But then he thought for a moment, asked for a pencil, scratched out the words 'Governor of Kyoto' on his card and asked the attendant to present it to the master again. Keichū looked at the card, smiled, and said 'Oh, is that Kitagaki? I want to see that fellow!'[11]

In the forest, without his usual social and psychological props, Ajātasattu becomes anxious and uneasy. The ego, faced with the night journey into the depths of consciousness, fears it is being led into a trap and to its destruction. This stage in the spiritual journey is akin to the 'dark night of the soul' of the Christian mystics. It is a changeover from deriving one's support and sense of identity from the environment to gaining it from the riches in the depths of one's own mind. Unfortunately, like someone swinging between trapezes, one has to let go of one's present perch and reach out into space if one is to reach the new source of support. In this sense the night journey is like a birth. One leaves the security of drawing one's nourishment from outside, and learns to function independently.

However, the everyday self does not have to make a leap of 'blind faith'. The King is led on by Jīvaka, his physician. In this symbolic reading of the story, Jīvaka represents the spiritual friend. Buddhism places tremendous importance on spiritual friendship – communication with people who have more knowledge of the path to freedom than you, who can encourage and inspire you when you feel you are lost in the forest of consciousness. Jīvaka visits the Buddha regularly. He knows from his own experience that the forest is not dangerous. Despite appearances to the contrary, he is certain that it is possible for its silence to conceal a great assembly of wisdom and compassion. So he can urge the King onwards, and give him confidence. We could also see Jīvaka as a guiding inner aspect of the King, an intuitive side that somehow knows there is more to consciousness than the superficial levels, and which can lead him, laden down as he is with his guilt, to a source of healing.

Jīvaka, the healer of bodies, leads the King to the Buddha, the healer of minds. In fact, the Buddha was sometimes called the Great Physician. One of his central teachings, the Four Noble Truths, is said to be based on ancient Indian medical formula. The Buddha identified the disease of humanity as unsatisfactoriness, the cause as craving, and the prognosis as excellent – a full cure with the state of Enlightenment – provided that the course of treatment of the Eightfold Path (right view, right emotion, right speech, right action, right livelihood, right effort, right concentration, and right meditation) was followed.

The King panics in the darkness (having left behind his attendants with their torches), but the encouragement of his spiritual friend gives him the faith and courage to continue. Finally he sees the torches of wisdom shining deep within the forest. He emerges from the trees, which symbolically form a maze or labyrinth, and arrives at a still space in the depths of consciousness. This deep level of the mind is silent – it usually gives no indication of its presence to the everyday ego. It makes no demands. It is simply there. But to contact it is to come home; to feel a sense of awe and wonder at the beauty, depth, and richness of the mind. So the King, seeing the great assembly of meditators with the Buddha at their heart, is overwhelmed by this revelation of the treasures of peace and wisdom that have been hidden in the depths of the forest. He is transformed by arriving at the centre of the maze of consciousness in this way. He gives up his old beliefs and goes for Refuge to the Buddha. He purifies himself of his terrible crime by openness and confession. And, contemplating the great assembly in meditation, he forgets himself and thinks instead of his son, wishing that he may experience such peace and contentment.

Here, unfortunately, there is a gap between the symbolic and the literal world. There is an irony in this story on the historical level, which is worthy of a Greek tragedy. Ajātasattu, who has killed his own father, Bimbisāra, feels guilt and remorse dragging at his mind, and longs for his son Udāyabhadda, whom he loves deeply, to know the happiness that his crime has denied him. Sadly, Ajātasattu's reign was brought to an end in about 459 BCE when he was killed in his turn by Prince Udāyabhadda, the son he so loved. And so the wheel of suffering continues to turn....

### Some Principles of Meditation

Whilst there are benefits to be gained by literally entering the forest, living in the forest fundamentally means venturing beyond egotistic security. To become truly free, we need to make an inner journey – leaving behind the safe palace of the surface level of our mind, and entering the inner forest of unexplored levels of consciousness. This is where the practice of meditation comes in. Meditation is a vast subject, and not something one can learn satisfactorily from books. However, it is central to the Buddhist path to freedom, as we saw from the major place it occupied in the Buddha's answer to Ajātasattu, so I shall say here a little about the principles of Buddhist meditation.

Ajātasattu could find no peace of mind on that full moon night because his extremely unethical behaviour in killing his father weighed on his mind. In outlining the path to freedom to the King, the Buddha talked about ethics before describing meditative states. This is because you can meditate successfully and consistently only on the basis of an ethical life. In fact, true meditation consists of a continuous flow of powerful, ethically positive states. We saw in Chapter 1 that the Buddhist precepts involve the development of qualities such as loving-kindness, generosity, contentment, truthfulness, and awareness. These qualities, which those on the Buddhist path to freedom aim to cultivate in everyday life, can be experienced especially strongly when we withdraw the mind from outside objects and concentrate inwardly. This allows us to experience these positive qualities undistracted by sense-impressions. More than that, it enables us to become more aware of our mental states and gently and steadily to work to cultivate and deepen these ethical qualities such as contentment and loving-kindness.

The word 'meditation' can be used in two senses: as the practice of working with the mind in order to clear away the obstacles to higher states of consciousness, and as the actual experience of those higher mental states. The Buddha outlines for the King the obstacles that stand between us and the meditative states of bliss and deep contentment. These are known in Buddhism as the five hindrances: desire for sense-experience, ill will, sloth and torpor, restlessness and anxiety, and doubt. It can be comforting to reflect that if we can just hold these five hindrances in abeyance for a little while we shall experience higher and more satisfying states of mind. While there is much that could be said about all five, and how to work with them, the meaning of the first four will be fairly obvious. Doubt is not so much to do with honest questioning as with an unwillingness to come to a conclusion, to make up one's mind and commit energy to the practice of meditation. The Buddha says that the basis for overcoming the hindrances is awareness of the senses and simplifying one's life. We shall look more at this advice in the next section.

The Buddha explains to Ajātasattu that once the hindrances have been overcome – at least temporarily – one enters meditation, in the sense of enjoying higher states of consciousness. This true meditation also has two aspects. The first is calming the mind and attaining increasingly concentrated states. These states, known as *jhāna* in Pāli (*dhyāna* in Sanskrit) are deeply enjoyable, and become increasingly refined and blissful. However, though they are a vast improvement on our usual states, they are only a temporary respite from unsatisfactoriness. To break out of suffering completely we need to cultivate the second kind of true meditation, through which we gain insight into the true nature of reality. Calming the mind and insight meditation work together. Through the former we become able to concentrate strongly and clearly, then we use this powerfully focused state to examine the nature particularly of our own mind and body, as the Buddha describes. Once we come to see the nature of reality, not just intellectually but in a flash of intuitive understanding based on a concentrated mind, we shall have reached the stage of Stream-entry, which sadly eluded Ajātasattu's grasp in his meeting with the Buddha.

*States of Mind and 'You Are What You Eat'*
While we may practise meditation regularly, can we really make a radical shift in our level of consciousness whilst living an otherwise unchanged life? In order to overcome the hindrances that block our entry to higher states, the Buddha mentions two factors we need to cultivate outside meditation. The first of these is that, at the very least, most of us will need to simplify our lives, to give ourselves some time and peace away from the bombardment of modern-day living. Ajātasattu had all the noise of his 500 elephants and their riders to distract him. Today we have a much greater barrage of information, noise, distractions, and demands hammering at our minds all the time. So, if we wish to hear what one writer calls 'the voice of the silence' we shall need to do whatever we can to live a simpler, less cluttered lifestyle, and to reduce the amount of every-day input.

These days, many people are concerned to ensure that what they put into their stomachs is healthy, and that they eat a well-balanced diet. But relatively few people give the same degree of thought to the diet on which they feed their minds. In the course of a day the mind of the average city-dweller munches indiscriminately through an indigestible mixture of ingredients. This may include a political row, a flood, and a couple of murders from the morning news bulletin; the faces or car bumpers of a thousand or so fellow com-muters; various bits of office gossip around the coffee machine; and a whole number of work issues to think about (and it's only mid-morning). By the end of a day of such non-stop force-feeding it is not surprising that many people feel mentally rather bloated and unwell. Nor should it come as a shock that when they sit down to snatch a few minutes' quiet at the end of the day their minds are too busy processing this unpalatable surfeit of material to be able to attain any degree of quiet and calm.

To help us improve our mental diet – and therefore our mental states – it is essential to practise 'guarding the gates of the senses' – the second of the Buddha's recommendations for overcoming the hindrances to meditation. This means staying aware and keeping the initiative in relation to the experiences and impressions to which we expose our minds. It will involve both reducing and refining what we take in. Firstly, we need to find ways of reducing the quantity of input. If we fed our bodies in the way we feed our minds most of us would have died of obesity long ago. Do we really need to fill our lives with wall-to-wall experience? Can we listen to ourselves rather than the radio or TV for once? In particular, can we learn to do one thing at a time, giving it all our attention? Then we need to look at the quality. Are we living on the mental equivalent of junk food? Are the experiences we take in fulfilling? Do they broaden our understanding of life and encourage us to become better, freer human beings? Or are they just intensifying our tendency to distract ourselves, to fill ourselves with pleasant experiences that never really satisfy us, like living on a diet of strawberry cheesecake? Lastly, we need to look at the assumptions, views, and opinions behind what we take in, keeping a sharp critical edge to our minds to question the values we are being offered by the magazines we read, the films we see, the people we spend time with.

Buddhism thinks of us having six senses. It sees the everyday mind as a sense that needs to be guarded like the others. Just as the eye deals in visual impressions and the ear in sounds, the everyday mind engages with memories, thoughts, and fantasies. Just as it is important to monitor what is coming in from outside, we need to pay attention to guarding the gate of the mind. We shall find that there is little we can do directly to dam the flow of thought. Plans, worries, pieces of music, powerful feelings, seemingly-random associations, and many other things flow continuously through us throughout the day. This endless stream carries all kinds of flotsam and jetsam from the profound to the tedious. Whilst we cannot usually control it, we can make the effort to be aware of it, and to see what aspects of it we are putting energy into. Those mental events that we reinforce by dwelling on them tend to become habitual. It is important to see whether we are creating positive habits or more mental shackles for ourselves.

*Time Away (and Leaving Altogether)*
As well as making a strong effort to guard the gates in the midst of everyday life, it will also be very helpful, if at all possible, to give ourselves some time away from our usual circumstances. At the risk of flogging the food analogy to death, this time away is like the

mental equivalent of a visit to a health farm, in which we allow the mind time to relax, and feed it a very light and healthy diet. There are various ways of doing this. We can go away on a meditation retreat, of which there are many organized by different Buddhist groups in the West these days. Alternatively, we can take some time alone, preferably away from home in natural surroundings. We can spend a day, weekend, week, month, or even longer, allowing our mind to calm and settle: spending time in meditation, as well as reflecting on our lives, and perhaps doing some reading that inspires us to follow the path to freedom. (Even with this kind of reading we need to be careful about quantity. More isn't usually better. One page that we reflect on and take to heart is worth a hundred that just wash over us.)

We may even need to think radically, to consider leaving our usual circumstances behind altogether. In our story, Ajātasattu is prevented from seeing the true nature of existence and finding his freedom because of the crime that weighs so heavily on his mind. His is a very extreme case, but sometimes much more ordinary circumstances can block our progress towards freedom. We may have a circle of friends who support and encourage us in following the ignoble quest – such as drinking or taking drugs. Or we may have a job where the values we are expected to uphold go against our beliefs. Clearly, at the time of the Buddha many people felt cramped and confined in their lives. They felt they had lost their freedom, lost the initiative to alter circumstances. So they re-established it by radical means. They left everything they knew and ventured into the forest. Obviously we must not do this in an irresponsible way. But we should not dismiss it as a possibility.

In any case we need to bear in mind that our present circumstances are temporary. Many people in ancient India saw that their existential situation was that they were wanderers through this world. Leaving home, their lives became demonstrations and reminders of this fact. Some of the meditations they practised helped to reinforce this awareness – particularly the contemplation of impermanence or death. After all, at death we shall leave behind all our surface concerns, even our own body, and – ready or not – we shall find ourselves venturing into the unknown. Reflecting on this fact helps us put into perspective our everyday concerns. It can also encourage us to give time to meditation and other methods that help us to find the centre of wisdom and peace within our own minds.

Whether or not our search for freedom leads us to change our external circumstances, internally a major revolution has to take place. We need to 'go forth' from basing our lives on the search for pleasure, gain, fame, and praise – all of which are impermanent and external. Then, even though we are living within society, we shall be outside it, in the sense of not sharing its values, and not being controlled by desire for success and approval. Once we have made the journey deep into our own minds and found the riches of states of profound meditation, we shall carry that peace and contentment into every situation in which we find ourselves.

# 4

# Beyond Bargaining

## *A Plot to Discredit the Buddhists*

According to tradition, the Buddha gained Enlightenment at the age of 35, and died at the age of 80. He spent the intervening 45 years moving around northern India, teaching people the way to freedom. Over the years, as he continued his tireless teaching, the number of his followers increased manyfold – both wanderers and those living the household life. As we saw in the last chapter, there were at that time many wanderers following different beliefs and teachers. The Buddha's success, and the consequent ease with which his wandering followers found help and support from the lay people, not surprisingly created a certain amount of envy among some of the followers of other teachers. This story concerns such a situation, and a conspiracy to ruin the reputation of the Buddha's followers.

We are once again in the great town of Sāvatthi, in Kosala, which we visited in Chapter 2. Sāvatthi is one of the main centres of the Buddha's teaching, and he and his followers are held in high esteem. Indeed they have the patronage of the King of Kosala, Pasenadi, who is probably the most powerful ruler in India. In addition, the Jeta Grove, a fine park a little way out of the city, has been bought for them by the rich businessman Anāthapiṇḍika. Many people are appreciative of the Buddha's teaching and are happy to provide him and his followers with everything they need, which – because the Buddhist wanderers are committed to lives of simplicity – is very little: robes and bowls, food, simple lodgings, and medicines.

The people's enthusiasm for the Buddha's teaching, and their appreciation of the conduct of his followers, inevitably means that, by contrast, the teachings and practices of other wanderers appear less satisfactory. As a result, wanderers following other teachers receive less respect, and it has become harder for them to find material support. For some of them this is very difficult to bear (which rather confirms the people's lower estimation of them).

The Buddha has tried to prevent other wanderers from suffering as a result of the popularity of his teaching. When he was staying among the Vajjians a general called Sīha, a leading supporter of the Jains, came to debate with him. The Buddha's teaching so impressed the general that he wished to become his disciple. But the Buddha advised him to consider such a step very carefully, as it would have consequences for the Jains. Eventually, General Sīha did become a Buddhist, but still the Buddha encouraged him to continue to support the Jains who were dependent on him.

Despite this, some of the other wanderers living in the Sāvatthi area become disgruntled, and resentful of this Buddhist cuckoo in their nest. When they meet together, much of their time is spent in jealous complaints about how the Buddha has spirited away their followers and taken the food out of their alms-bowls. Eventually, a small group of them, even more malcontent than the rest, decide on drastic measures to destroy their Buddhist competitors' image. They meet in secret to decide what is to be done, and devise a plan.

As step one, they go to talk to one of their female companions, called Sundarī. Her name means 'beautiful', and she is an attractive and open-hearted young woman. The group ask Sundarī to do them a favour. She is happy to consent, without hearing what the favour is, because she would gladly do anything for her kinsmen. However, the favour is quite a simple one. The group simply ask Sundarī to regularly visit the park where the Buddhist wanderers are staying. Sundarī is happy to do as she is asked. Her friends add one more point: can she be sure to visit the Jeta Grove in a conspicuous way, so that people notice her doing so? (This will not be difficult, as Sundarī lives up to her name.) Sundarī agrees to this condition too, without even asking what it is all about.

People soon become used to seeing the attractive young wanderer visiting the Jeta Grove. She is there so often, on one pretext or another, that some even wonder if she is interested in the Buddha's teaching. After a few weeks of this, the group thank Sundarī for what she has done. She is happy to have been of service, though she cannot see how what she has done has benefited anyone. The group assure her that she has been of help, and could now do them an even greater favour if she will meet them that evening, near the Jeta Grove. Sundarī is nervous of wandering around after sunset, so one of the group agrees to accompany her.

With her escort, Sundarī makes her way to the appointed place with a light heart, happy at the thought that she may be of further service to her fellow wanderers. When they arrive at the rendezvous, three of her kinsmen are waiting. She asks them what further favour she can do for them. In response, her escort suddenly puts his hand over her mouth, and the others advance upon her. Poor Sundarī is killed by the fellow wanderers she had been so happy to help. Then, under cover of darkness, a couple of them take her body to the Jeta Grove and bury it in a ditch.

The next day the group seek an audience with Pasenadi. They complain to him that Sundarī has disappeared, and they are afraid she may have come to harm. The King asks the distressed group if they have any suspicions as to where she might be. They have no idea. Except, now they come to think of it, in the weeks before she disappeared Sundarī had taken it into her head to go visiting the Jeta Grove. Perhaps she might be there.... The King gives them permission to scour the Grove. At this the wanderers gather together as many people as possible and make their way to their rivals' stronghold. The Buddhists are naturally surprised to have such a crowd descend upon them. However, when it is explained that Pasenadi has given the group permission to search for their kinswoman, the Buddhists allow them to do so. The group make a great show of searching the Grove. After some time, amid a great clamour, they manage to 'discover' poor Sundarī's corpse in the ditch.

The group make as much capital out of their find as they can. They put the body on a litter, and parade it around Sāvatthi. As they do so, they complain bitterly to everyone they meet, saying, 'Look what these followers of Gotama have done! These shameless hypocrites claim to be living pure lives as homeless wanderers, but actually they have abandoned any peace of mind or purity. How could a man, having slept with a woman, kill her in this way?' By this means they do everything they can to incite the townspeople to indignation.

The Buddha's followers, going into Sāvatthi next morning to beg for food, suddenly find themselves taunted and vilified by people repeating the group's insults and accusations. Having gathered what food is to be had – and from some quarters supplies have completely dried up – the Buddhists return to the Jeta Grove, some of the newer wanderers looking pale and shaken.

Naturally they go to the Buddha and tell him of the abuse they have encountered in the city. The Buddha's response is calm and measured. He predicts that, if it is handled in the right way, the uproar will not last long, that it will subside in a week. Nonetheless, some of his followers are still very anxious, others are angry at being treated so unjustly. The Buddha urges all of them to reply patiently to the abuse and criticism. He tells them to respond to their accusers by asserting the serious consequences of lying or hiding the truth. In this way they will put themselves on oath: that they have spoken the truth when they deny all knowledge of Sundarī's murder.

Over the next few days, when the townspeople again abuse them, the Buddhists reply gently in the way taught them by the Buddha. The calm demeanour of the Buddhists, and the way in which they have put themselves on oath to tell the truth, begins to sway the opinion of the townspeople. They start doubting if the Buddhists are guilty of the crime they were charged with by the other wanderers. Within a week, as the Buddha predicted, his followers meet with no more accusations. Very soon the former high opinion that many people in Sāvatthi had of the Buddhists is restored.

Some of his followers express their surprise to the Buddha at how quickly the furore has died away. Reflecting on the recent events, he sums up the lesson to be learned from them in a verse:

> *Folk unrestrained pierce through (a man) with words*
> *As an elephant with arrows in a fight.*
> *Hearing the utterance of bitter speech*
> *Let a monk bear it unperturbed at heart.*[12]

### Taking Offence and the Reciprocal Relationship

What can we draw from this story and the Buddha's advice to his followers? Ringing clearly through it is a strong injunction to practise patience. At Sāvatthi the Buddha's followers could have responded with anger and upset at being unjustly accused. They might have started making counter-accusations against the other wanderers. The incident would then have escalated, and would certainly not have died away in seven days. If we follow the news, we shall find that very frequently some group or individual is reported as being very angry at the way they have been treated, or at some insensitive remark made about them. Sometimes religious groups feel they are entitled to righteous indignation at some offence which has been offered to their beliefs. From a Buddhist point of view this whole tendency to anger, righteous indignation, and taking offence is unhelpful, and leads to more suffering. The Buddhist ideal is to maintain a positive feeling even for those who are critical or abusive, and to respond objectively to what they say: acknowledging what is true and pointing out what is untrue in a measured way.

This story has wider implications. Practising patience in the face of criticism is one example of a much wider principle which is crucial to the whole quest for freedom. This chapter is entitled 'Beyond Bargaining' because what this story fundamentally shows is that to become truly free we need to go beyond what I call the reciprocal relationship.

What is this 'reciprocal relationship'? Let us first be clear how I am using the word 'reciprocal'. It can mean just 'mutual', but here I mean it in the sense of a relationship in which things are done (or not done) *in return for* something else. Suppose I invite you to dinner. You might return the invitation by inviting me to lunch. In this way you reciprocate – you give me something equivalent to what I have given you.

Whilst this can be a perfectly reasonable way to operate, certain kinds of reciprocal relationship are limiting and unhelpful. Let us try to imagine the train of thought of one of the Buddhist wanderers entering Sāvatthi, who does *not* manage to follow the Buddha's injunction, who does produce thoughts of ill will towards the townspeople who are abusing him. His internal dialogue probably runs along these lines: 'Here am I, a wanderer. I've left my home in search of the truth. I am completely blameless of Sundarī's murder. I'm trying to practise harmlessness and non-violence – love for the world. And what do I get in return? False accusations and abuse!'

What is going on here? The wanderer's hurt and anger is based upon the idea that there is, or there should be, some kind of reciprocal relationship between the way he acts and how people treat him. But on this occasion the reciprocal relationship has been broken by the accusing townspeople. The wanderer feels he has done nothing to deserve this treatment, so he feels a 'righteous' or 'justified' anger. The Buddha very clearly disowned this kind of thinking in many of his teachings.

### Leaving the World of the Manu

We can widen out from this example, and the Buddha's condemnation of taking offence, to derive a more general principle. Someone following the path to freedom needs to give up thinking in terms of a reciprocal relationship between what they give and what they receive. Looking for a correlation between what you are entitled to and what you should give to others will cause you suffering and block your progress on the path to freedom.

You might well question this statement, arguing that reciprocal relationships are fundamental and necessary to the operation of human societies. After all, as a member of society, you are endowed with certain rights and privileges, which are bestowed on you by society provided you operate within its norms and carry out your duties as a citizen. There is a direct relationship between giving and receiving.

Whilst this is true on its own level, it is a framework of thought that is superseded once we enter upon the path to freedom. There is a teaching found in the Tibetan tradition that can help us here. Buddhism has a perspective which encompasses aeons. It sees world systems evolving and then disappearing. A Buddha is the first person to gain Enlightenment in a particular era. However, according to this tradition, before a Buddha can appear and teach the Dharma there must first be a *manu*, who helps to set up the conditions for a society in which Enlightenment can be attained. The manu is a primordial lawgiver, who lays down the principles of justice and fairness for society. (Here the tradition uses 'manu' to cover a type of individual, or even an archetype. The Indian *Manusmriti*, a text which was fundamental in determining how Indian society developed, includes many manifestly unjust laws which discriminated against the so-called 'untouchables'.) These laws and principles are essential if society is to cohere at all. All healthy societies are underpinned by concepts of fairness and respect for the rule of law. Nonetheless, necessary as it is, the world of the manu is clearly founded on reciprocal relationship. When you step on the path to freedom you move from the sphere of the manu to that of the Buddha. The latter, though based on the work of the manu, goes beyond it. The manu deals with group members; the Buddha with individuals.

In the sphere of the manu, if someone mistreats you or robs you, you are entitled through the institutions of law to recover what you have lost and to take a form of institutionalized revenge. The domain of the manu is based on the maxim 'Do as you have been done to.' The world of the manu in the modern West is that of the Old Testament, softened by a degree of liberalism, but basically still operating on the basis of 'an eye for an eye, and a tooth for a tooth'. But when we start searching for true freedom, our whole perspective changes. As part of Going for Refuge we enter a sangha, a free association of individuals striving to become free. We try as far as we can to leave behind the world of the manu, to leave behind the reciprocal relationship. The only law possible among true followers of the path to freedom is the law of loving-kindness.

*The Reciprocal Relationship Between Stimulus and Response*
Leaving behind the world of the manu, one gives up the assumptions of mundane life, and starts out on the freedom trail. But what is the essential nature of the process by which we are caught up in mundane life? All the time our five senses are receiving stimuli, and our mind is constantly producing a flow of ideas, memories, and imaginings. All these stimuli have feelings associated with them: pleasant, painful, or neutral. There is no problem with this in itself, but all too often we respond to these feelings automatically. If the stimulus is unpleasant we react with aversion, we either pull away or go on the offensive. If it is pleasant we react with craving, we move towards it (literally or metaphorically). Therefore, until we start out on the path to freedom by working on our minds, there will be a close reciprocal relationship between stimulus and response, what we are given and what we give. As with getting cash from a bank's automatic teller, the response will be stereotyped and predictable because it is almost totally conditioned by what is given in the environment. In fact we can say that the reciprocal relationship is the conditioned relationship.

To move on to the path to freedom, however, we have to begin to break this reciprocal relationship between what we receive and what we give. In response to the unpleasant feeling when we are faced with hatred, say, instead of automatically producing hatred we try to produce loving-kindness, or patience, or equanimity. By doing so, we become increasingly spontaneous and less conditioned by the world. If we keep doing this, we shall eventually arrive at a point on the path to freedom where however strong the stimulus, even if we are unjustly accused of murder, we no longer play the reciprocal game. Even if we are unfairly criticized or caused pain, it will not occur to us to respond in kind. At that point, we will have broken the chains of the reciprocal relationship and immeasurably widened the sphere of our freedom.

### Examples of the Reciprocal Relationship

So far, this may have sounded interesting but a little theoretical. So it is time to spell out some of the practical implications. For our quest for freedom to be successful, we need to make two fundamental shifts in attitude. First, we need to give up all thinking based on the reciprocal relationship between what we give and what we receive. And second (a corollary of the first but so important that it needs to be stated separately), we need to be prepared to give freely without expecting anything in return.

Let's go into this in more detail. We'll start by exploring the idea that we have to give up all thinking based on there being a reciprocal relationship between what we give and what we receive. Clearly, to do this will require a very thoroughgoing and radical examination of our attitudes and our habitual modes of thought, because this way of operating is subtle and all-pervasive. Here are a few examples of the kind of thinking I am questioning. I cannot begin to exhaust the possibilities, which are endless.

*Nobody else does X, so why should I?* as in 'Nobody else washes up after themselves, so why should I?' You could imagine one of the Buddhist wanderers in Sāvatthi who failed to follow the Buddha's advice to be calm and patient. They might lose their temper, justifying it with the thought, 'None of these townspeople is treating me with any respect or politeness, so why should I be patient or polite to them?' When you think in that way or make that kind of statement, you as an individual are not deciding for yourself what is the right thing to do. You are simply letting what you give be determined by others' lack of giving. This means there will be no consistency to your actions. They are not based on unchanging principles but are swayed by the vagaries of the actions of those around you. Thus you are, in effect, controlled by your environment, and have lost your freedom.

*I do X, so why don't you?* as in 'I give up two evenings a week to help run this charity, so why can't you?' This may be a legitimate statement, if you are simply pointing out to someone that you can do something, and there is nothing exceptional about you, so they could also do it. But usually behind 'If I do X why don't you?' lurks a kind of tit for tat feeling. '*I* am giving in this way, so you should feel guilty about not giving in this way too.' Again you could imagine a Buddhist wanderer bursting out in frustration against his critics: 'I try to practise kindly speech, and to give people the benefit of the doubt. So why can't you?' Lurking behind this kind of thinking is often: 'Why can't everyone be more like me?' In other words, why can't everyone give in the same way that I give? So again you are looking for a reciprocal relationship between what you give and what others should give. This is not usually a very productive attitude and fails to see people as individuals. Indeed, expecting people to be like ourselves (when after all they are like *themselves*) is probably the murky pool in which most of this negative thinking in terms of reciprocal relationships is spawned.

*I'll give you X if you'll give me Y.* In a way, this statement sums up the classic reciprocal relationship. Many sexual relationships have elements of this kind of trade-off, in which, sadly, sex and affection can become bargaining counters. Both parties are prepared to give only if they are given to, and this inevitably creates tension. The image that for me crystallizes the whole reciprocal relationship in the negative sense is one of those playground scenes where John has taken Errol's calculator and in response Errol has picked up John's mobile phone. What happens next? They are both prepared to give, but only if they get their own items back. So they move cautiously towards each other, each trying to make sure they will receive before they are prepared to let go and give. This tense and suspicious reaching out, being prepared to give but also looking for the opportunity to grab what one wants, symbolizes this whole reciprocal relationship. We find it in personal relationships, and all too clearly in politics.

This is not to deny that under certain circumstances if I give a newsagent some money and they give me a newspaper, that is legitimate and useful. But all transactions of that type belong to the world of the manu, and – as we shall see later – wherever possible the spiritual aspirant just gives. There are also, by the way, negative versions of 'I'll give you X if you'll give me Y', as in 'If you criticize me, I'll give you so much trouble you'll wish you hadn't bothered.' Faced with a threat or some harm to ourselves, we respond with sanctions or violence. Again, simply to 'turn the other cheek' may not be the wisest thing to do. If someone is acting in a bullying and manipulative way, allowing them to achieve their ends simply gives them the message that using power is a successful life-strategy. We may need to stand up to people who act in such a way and refuse to give them what they want. However, this should be done out of concern for them and ourselves, not because we have descended to their level and wish to spite them in return for their ill treatment of us.

*If I am not given X, I won't give you Y.* Some people live their whole lives based on this attitude. 'I wasn't given what I needed as a child, therefore I am not really going to give to anybody until I get what I need.' Unfortunately the God of popular and unsubtle Christianity appears to operate in this way too: 'If you do not give me your love and devotion for having created you, I am not going to let you into Heaven.' The wanderers of other sects in our story are not given respect or appreciation, so they will not give any to the Buddha's followers. In fact they go a stage further, into a very vicious version of 'If I am not given X, I'll make sure that no one else receives it either.'

*Everyone else does X, so I suppose I shall have to as well,* as in 'Everyone else has agreed to stop eating battery eggs, so I suppose I shall have to as well.' Even though your decision may be a good one, in all these examples the issue is one of motivation. In this case you give up your individuality, your own judgement, because you relate your decision to that of others and feel obliged to do what they do. Perhaps some of the Buddha's newer followers thought it would be better to argue back to the townspeople, and only kept quiet or repeated the Buddha's suggested response out of fear that other disciples would criticize them. This sub-individual attitude, in which one goes along with the group out of fear of losing its approval, needs to be carefully distinguished from deferring to others out of respect for their judgement, which can be a very positive motivation.

A small example of this negative tendency that I found within myself a few years back was that somebody would write me a letter and sign it 'with much love, so-and-so'. When I wrote back to them, I felt I had to respond in kind by putting 'with much love, Vessantara'. Eventually I realized that by doing so I was being constrained by what the other person wrote, and at times my reciprocal show of affection was dishonest. Naturally I take into account that people use these expressions in different ways, but these days if I honestly do not feel so strongly for that person I reply 'With best wishes, Vessantara'.

*You cannot criticize me for X, because you do Y,* as in 'You cannot criticize me for being late for work because you take such long lunch breaks.' A Buddhist wanderer could have rounded upon the Sāvatthi householders, saying, 'How dare you criticize me for being a hypocrite when you aren't making any efforts yourself, and are just immersed in worldly life!' You can imagine how well that would have gone down. This kind of reciprocal thinking causes more trouble in social situations – even between people practising the Dharma together – than almost any other. If someone does give you some criticism, it never helps to criticize them back. If you do so the situation becomes one of futile tit for tat: 'If you are going to criticize me, I'm going to list my grievances about you.' If you respond with criticism, you usually spark off an escalating series of recriminations. If someone criticizes you, even if you know that their behaviour is more open to criticism than yours, you should consider what they say on its merits, and accept it if is true. On a separate occasion, you may gently point out that they also sometimes act in unhelpful ways. Tying the two together into a reciprocal relationship always causes trouble and bad feeling.

*I'd better not say anything to them about X, because they might criticize me for Y.* This is the other side of the coin, as in 'I won't criticize him for going out drinking in case he criticizes me for being extravagant with money.' You often find more than one person in a situation thinking in this way. Two or more people may collude together, tacitly agreeing not to notice each other's unhelpful behaviour so that they can all carry on doing what they like. If you come upon a situation among Dharma practitioners that feels rather dead, where there is not much energy moving, then you can suspect that people have sunk into this kind of collusive reciprocal relationship, where they are not going to raise issues with one another for fear of being questioned themselves.

I could carry on multiplying examples, but I trust I have said enough to make clear what I mean here by a reciprocal relationship, in the negative sense. The reciprocal relationship is the conditioned relationship, where what you give and take is governed by what others are giving and taking. It is the tit for tat, you scratch my back and I'll scratch yours, relationship. It is the mode of thinking that underlies all the principles of mundane life, and it is deeply ingrained in all of us. In every example I have given, the thinking is based on gross or subtle forms of relating in terms of power. One of our tasks, having embarked on the path to freedom, is to dump all this baggage of thinking in reciprocal terms, constantly making some kind of tie-up between giving and receiving. In order to become free individuals we need to break out of the reciprocal relationship and all other ways in which we relate to others, crudely or subtly, in terms of power.

### Give What You Can, Take What You Need?

Now it is time to look at the second fundamental shift in attitude I mentioned. This we saw is the corollary of giving up thinking in reciprocal terms: that we need to be prepared to give freely without expecting anything in return. From a Buddhist point of view even the Marxist slogan: 'Give what you can, take what you need,' is not radical enough. Probably the ideal motto for a Buddhist sangha would be 'Give what you can.' Full stop. But perhaps that is not very realistic, so I had better propose: 'Give what you can, ask for whatever you need in order to enable you to continue to give.' That would be an acceptable reciprocal relationship, if we can call it that, between giving and receiving.

This was the position of the Buddha and his immediate disciples. The Buddha does not seem to have expected to be fed – he did not remind people as he went on his alms-round that he had taught so much Dharma, and given so much to the world, that he was entitled to be supported. He simply poured out the Dharma like golden rain on all people equally, and went silently from house to house with his alms-bowl. And if some days he did not get what he needed and he went hungry, he did not complain. So when you start out on the Buddhist path to freedom, you aspire to give freely to the world with no strings attached. Ideally, all you hope for from the world is that it will enable you to satisfy your basic material needs so that you will be able to continue to help it.

In taking this approach to life you will be very out of step with surrounding society. The language of rights and entitlements is everywhere these days. On its own level, in the world of the manu, this is reasonable enough. I am not denying that there are certain rights with which a society ought to endow its citizens, such as the right to a fair trial, and which should be campaigned for if necessary (although many people these days seem much keener on demanding their rights than on fulfilling their responsibilities as citizens). However, when you move from the world of the manu to the world of the Buddha, and start looking at your existential situation from that wider perspective, you see that the universe confers no rights on sentient beings and knows nothing of their entitlements. You recognize that you can never completely rely on having your needs met, because that would be to expect mundane life – *saṁsāra* in Pāli – to give you what you want. By its nature, saṁsāra is bound to be unreliable in satisfying your needs. The only contract that saṁsāra guarantees to fulfil is to provide a continuous experience of what Buddhism calls the 'three marks', which are characteristics of all mundane experience: impermanence, unsatisfactoriness, and lack of inherent existence. It will fulfil that contract perfectly. The person committed to true freedom sees this clearly, which is why they 'go forth from saṁsāra', to use traditional terminology. Going forth means no longer expecting the mundane to satisfy your needs. Seeing this, the person who has gone forth, who has gone for Refuge, looks only to the Three Jewels to satisfy them.

Of course, this does not mean that if you have gone for Refuge and you need a pair of shoes, you may not go to a shoe shop. It means that you no longer finally *rely* on anything but the Three Jewels. You see everything else as unreliable. So you are not surprised or disappointed when the shop is closed, or nothing fits. After all, that is saṁsāra. I think it is worth reflecting on how often we expect saṁsāra to give us what we need and are disappointed, even though we know that everything changes so that nothing mundane is 100% reliable. In all aspects of life things will go wrong, and our needs will not be met.

Whilst we cannot rely on mundane affairs to go right for us, we can at least try to be a source of steady kindness and confidence for the world. Through practising the precepts we can become an increasingly trustworthy force for good for those with whom we come into contact. Because we are committed to embodying the values of kindness, generosity, contentment, truthfulness, and awareness, people will trust us not to use power or manipulation. For us, following the precepts will gradually break the reciprocal relationship between what we give to the world and what we expect from it. Even if others are causing harm or using power to get their way, we don't join in. Whether or not others are grabbing what they can, we try to keep a generous attitude. Even if others are being manipulative to get their own way sexually, we don't play those games. Even if others are lying and swearing that black is white and all the other colours of the rainbow, we try to hold to the truth. Even if everyone else is drowning their sorrows, we work to keep awake and aware.

None of this is done in a 'holier than thou' way. That would be just another subtle form of reciprocal thinking, by which we indirectly reinforced our position in relation to others. Ideally we practise kindness, generosity, contentment, truthfulness, and mindfulness because we believe in them, because they bring us happiness, and because they are a gift to the world.

### Gratitude and 'Keeping Score'
In describing the dangers of thinking in terms of a reciprocal relationship between what you are prepared to give and the actions of others I am not denying the importance of gratitude. It is a beautiful and important quality. On the path to freedom, generosity sparks off more generosity. This is a natural process, between people whose hearts are open. It has nothing to do with 'keeping the accounts square'. Between two people on that rainbow way, generosity as an expression of openness sparks off more openness, but nobody keeps score.

Gratitude is a spiritual quality, whereas what I call 'keeping score' is part of the negative reciprocal relationship in the world of the manu. Put simply, when someone gives something to you there are two possible responses. You can keep your heart closed to them and keep score, in which case you feel in debt to that person. You may even feel subtly guilty or resentful that they have made you indebted to them. Or, not wishing to be put under an obligation to them, you quickly forget or dismiss their generosity to you – which means your heart is not affected by their kindness or their love for you. All this is the reciprocal relationship.

Alternatively, when someone opens themselves to you and gives, you can open your heart in response. Their giving, taken into your heart, gives birth to gratitude and sparks off further gratitude and further giving. And this process can carry on indefinitely between the two of you, or even more than two of you, in which case a spiral dance can begin, a soaring dance like eagles circling and leading one another higher and higher into the sky.

I am aware, painfully so at times, that it is hard to live up to this ideal. As people still on the early stages of the path to freedom, this gratitude and spontaneous generosity may not come naturally to us. We shall find it hard to give to people and expect nothing back, harder still at times when we receive nothing back. We shall have to work at it as a practice. It will be difficult for us to do until we arrive at the point that Gotamī came to, of Stream-entry. Even then, there will be resistance. However, as we continue along the transcendental path we shall eventually reach a point where, although our lives have become an outpouring of generosity, we shall give with no sense of there being a giver, a receiver, or a gift. This is what the Buddhist texts concerning the Perfection of Wisdom tell us. Hence there will be no sense of a reciprocal relationship between a giver and a receiver. Perhaps, as long as we feel ourselves to be a fixed subject giving to an object, however refined that feeling may be, there will always be some element of reciprocality, a subtle desire for the object to give us some return on our giving.

Though it may be difficult for us to break the reciprocal relationship and give freely and unconditionally, it is at least good to be clear that that is the ideal at which we are aiming, that is where the path to freedom leads. We can at least make a start by trying to give without feeling that we are putting the other person under any obligation to us, and to receive without feeling a guilty obligation to give back (or, if we are not in a position to reciprocate, not allowing ourselves fully to receive what has been given to us).

We can also try to become more conscious of our tendency to think in terms of tit for tat: 'If I give this, you should give that, if I do not give this, then....' or 'If they do not give this, then I will not give that,' and so on – tying together our giving and receiving with that of other people. We can work to catch ourselves thinking in this way, rationalizing or justifying our actions in terms of a reciprocal relationship between what we should give and what we are 'entitled' to receive. When we see these patterns of thought in ourselves, we can take the initiative by giving, by going out to people. In this way we shall initiate positive changes in the situations and relationships in which we are involved.

The points I have been making are seen most clearly in the arena of friendship. Some people see the process of making friendships as a reciprocal relationship. They wait for someone to be a friend to them, at which point they are prepared to give friendship in return. If nobody makes friendly overtures to them, they complain that they have no friends. When you step beyond the reciprocal relationship, you start to go out yourself, initiating the process of being a friend to people. When you do this, you will soon find you have plenty of friends.

### Levels of Giving

We have come a long way in this chapter. We could also look at the ground we have covered from another angle, by identifying three levels of giving: the level of the mundane – of the manu – before we set out on the path to freedom, the level of the path up to Stream-entry, and then the transcendental level.

In the world of the manu, you always give 'because' – and that 'because' springs from a conditioned relationship between subject and object. What you give is decided by what you have been given, or what you hope or expect to receive.

Once you venture on to the lower stages of the path to freedom you try as far as possible just to give. It is still giving 'because' but at least it is because you are being moved by an ideal, by the promptings of loving-kindness, by an intuition of freedom, rather than because you have to, because you are in a reciprocal relationship with the object.

Finally we come to the level of Stream-entry and beyond, where you are in touch with the true nature of things. Increasingly, as you follow the transcendental path, there is less idea of giving or receiving. Someone who has reached this level does not give 'because'. Or, if there is a 'because' attached to their giving, then the person who is far advanced on the path will tell you that they give because beings suffer and someone has to help. Or that they give because an act of giving, freely carried out, expecting nothing, is the most beautiful and satisfying act in the universe. Finally, however, they give for no reason, because giving has become as natural to them as breathing.

### The Example of the Tortured Wanderer

Sundarī's sad death, and the ensuing events at Sāvatthi, have provoked a number of reflections. They have pointed out the need to avoid conditioned relationships based on a reciprocal relationship between how we are treated by the world, and how we treat it. They have warned us to be on the lookout for all the ways of thinking that we may have carried on to the path, based on that type of relationship. They have highlighted the fact that on the path to freedom we need to cease relying on – having unrealistic expectations of – the mundane. And they have shown us the beauty of an attitude based on free giving.

Having seen all this, let's return to our starting point: to patience and forbearance, for we need to take one further step if we are to understand the full meaning of the story. In his verse, the Buddha speaks only of bearing abuse 'unperturbed at heart'. Patience in Buddhism is often compared to armour, which wards off attack. This can convey an impression of this quality as a kind of long-suffering endurance. However, good though this kind of passive forbearance may be, there is only limited freedom in simply remaining inactive, like a tortoise inside its shell. The patience we are looking to develop is not stolid indifference but a dynamic force, powered by loving-kindness. Much Buddhist practice, in meditation and in other ways, is devoted to fanning the flames of loving-kindness for all living beings. The energy of this loving-kindness eventually becomes so strong that it overpowers any negative responses we might have to unpleasant people and situations. When we respond with loving-kindness regardless of how others treat us then we shall have broken the chains of the reciprocal relationship for ever.

From the Buddhist point of view, patience and loving-kindness are not just to be applied in the face of criticism or abuse, but even in the face of violence. In one of his teachings to a man called Moliya-Phagguna the Buddha asks his hearers to imagine that one of his male wandering followers has been caught by bandits. These bandits take hold of him, and tie him down. They then bring a two-handed saw and start to saw him limb from limb. Now, says the Buddha, if that wanderer, as he was being hewn into pieces, should harbour any thoughts of ill will against his tormentors, he would not be acting as my disciple, he would not be following my teaching.[13]

If we bring the example up to date, and imagine someone being tortured by the agents of a repressive regime, we begin to feel the force of the statement the Buddha is making, and its universal applicability – that even if you are being tortured through no fault of your own, if you harbour any feeling of ill will towards those who are harming you, you are not following the Dharma, not moving towards freedom.

This is a very demanding ideal indeed. However, there are present-day examples of some Tibetan monks and nuns ill-treated by the Chinese who managed to hold to the Buddha's teaching. They suffered great physical pain and privation, but bore it all with peaceful hearts. Such people are freer than their jailers and torturers. They have gone beyond thoughts of a reciprocal relationship between themselves and the world. They give loving-kindness to their tormentors regardless of the pain they are inflicting. Perhaps there often passes through the minds of such people one of the first pieces of the Buddha's teaching they ever heard. It is a simple verse which, if we can allow its implications to permeate our being, will begin to dissolve away all thoughts of the reciprocal relationship. It runs

*Hatred does not cease by hatred;*
*Hatred ceases only by love.*[14]

# PART THREE

# Tibetan Buddhism

# 5

# Exchange is No Robbery

*Riding the Copper Horse*

This true story takes us to a small Chinese town, in the first half of the nineteenth century. A crowd has gathered on the corner of an anonymous-looking street. In the centre of the crowd a struggling man is being tied to a strange horse – not an animal of flesh and blood, but a horse made of copper. The man is sweating profusely, in a state of complete panic, pleading for mercy to the officials at the front of the crowd.

The man on the copper horse is a convicted thief, but at first it is hard to see why he should be so beside himself with fear. He is not about to be pilloried, for although the crowd is jeering, none of them is holding any missiles. However, once the captive has been firmly tied to the horse, one of the officials sets light to a torch. If we examine the horse more closely we shall see that this is a steed that nobody would want to ride. It has a hollow belly, within which is stacked a large heap of wood. The purpose of the lighted torch is now clear, and the man's terror becomes understandable. This is no pillorying; it is an execution. The fire will burn up inside the hollow frame of the horse, and the copper will become red hot. The rider will die a prolonged and tortured death.

The flaming torch is brandished aloft for the crowd, and above all the rider, to see. His pleas gain an increased desperation, his whole body taut against its restraints. Nevertheless, the torchbearer steps forward to carry out the sentence. Suddenly, someone pushes to the front of the crowd. He is a foreigner, wearing a *chuba* – the common attire of Tibetans. The stranger calls out to the official to wait. All eyes turn to him. He confesses that the man on the horse is not guilty, and that he himself committed the crimes for which an innocent man is about to be put to death.

Naturally this causes a great commotion. The man on the horse looks at the stranger wide-eyed, seemingly so panic stricken that he can barely comprehend what is being said. The officials, however, understand very well. Informed that they were about to execute the wrong man, they are happy to rectify their mistake. They release the trembling man from the copper horse, lay hands on the unresisting foreigner, and force him to mount the steed that will carry him to the land of the dead.

The crowd jeer and bay for blood with renewed intensity, stung by the thought that the real thief, this foreigner, had nearly allowed a local man to go to his death unjustly. Once the new victim has been tied to the horse, the flaming torch is again raised to the crowd. However, the eyes of the stranger do not follow it, nor does he cry out for mercy. His gaze is directed upwards, into the sky in front of him.

The torch is held under the horse, the kindling catches, and flames soon begin to lick upwards within its hollow belly. There are anticipatory cries from the crowd, but the man does not squirm or shuffle. He continues to sit bolt upright. Minutes pass and the fire burns more strongly, until those near the front of the crowd can feel the heat given off by the copper horse. However, now there is no exultation, and no more jeering. A strange silence has fallen over everyone. For, despite the searing heat and what it must be doing to his body, the man on the horse continues to sit erect, unmoving, like an equestrian statue, his eyes fixed on the sky as if on some distant star which is guiding him home. It is the most dignified death anyone present has ever witnessed.

Meanwhile, in their lodgings a few streets away, two other Tibetans are becoming increasingly concerned. Their companion, who had gone to take a short walk around the town, has not returned. Eventually they decide to go out and search for him. Finding no sign of their companion, they start enquiring after him from passers-by. It is a small enough place, and it is not long before they meet someone returning from the execution. The man looks at them suspiciously – surely these two are the Tibetan thief's accomplices?

However, he takes satisfaction in recounting to these foreigners the story of how their companion had nearly allowed an innocent man to be executed as a thief, only coming forward at the last moment to admit his guilt. Mind you, the fellow had made an extraordinary and dignified end on the copper horse....

The two Tibetans look at one another, devastated and awe-struck, realizing what has happened. They have only just arrived in this place with their beloved spiritual teacher, Dola Jigme Kalzang. On his walk he must have seen the execution about to take place. A great-hearted man, kindness itself, he could not have borne to see any human being suffer so much. Seeing no other way to prevent what was to happen, he had stepped forward and claimed to have committed the crimes himself. Thus he had given up his life for someone he had never met before, a foreigner, a thief. Transcending torture, he had died an awesome death, in deep meditation, upon the copper horse.

### The Heart of Tibetan Buddhism

With this story we have left behind the Pāli Canon and moved into the world of Tibetan Buddhism. This is an extremely rich expression of the Dharma, for over the centuries many thousands of texts and practices were brought to Tibet from India and Central Asia. In Tibet these treasures were preserved and practised long after they had been destroyed by Muslim invaders in their countries of origin. In 1959, when the Chinese took complete control of Tibet, there was an exodus of lamas to India and Nepal, taking with them whatever texts and religious objects they could carry as they fled for their lives. Thus the wheel turned full circle, with Buddhist texts and practices returning over the Himalayas. From there, to our great benefit, they are being spread around the world.

The aim of followers of all schools of Tibetan Buddhism is to follow the path of the Bodhisattva. This Sanskrit term, which literally means 'enlightenment being', connotes someone who is bent on achieving total freedom not for their own sake but for the sake of all that lives. Bodhisattvas are so moved by the suffering they see all around them that their deepest wish is to put an end to it entirely. However, they reflect that as long as they remain unenlightened they will be of only limited help to other beings – it will be a case, in spiritual terms, of the blind leading the blind. So they commit themselves to becoming a Buddha, totally Enlightened and free. Having achieved that state of wisdom and compassion, peace and energy, they will then be in the best possible position to help all living beings.

Early Buddhism, which we have been looking at in the previous three chapters, did not use the term 'Bodhisattva' ('Bodhisatta' in Pāli) except to refer to the Buddha in his previous lives. In the centuries after the Buddha's death, an Enlightened person was called an Arhant – a 'worthy one'.[15] At this stage of the development of Buddhism, the Arhant ideal was also one of gaining the fullness of both wisdom and compassion. For example, the Buddha's advice to his first sixty Arhant disciples was to wander in the world 'for the profit of the many, for the bliss of the many, out of compassion for the world'.[16] But over the centuries following the Buddha's death, this ideal of becoming an Arhant was narrowed down in some quarters, becoming identified only with finding one's own personal liberation from suffering. Thus a further definition of the goal of the spiritual life in its fullness became necessary. In response, the Mahā-yāna – 'Great Way' – movement propounded the ideal of the Bodhi-sattva, who is explicitly committed to striving for wisdom and compassion to gain Enlightenment for the sake of all living beings, and to work for their benefit until all have put an end to suffering. It is this ideal that stands at the heart of Tibetan Buddhism.

The true story of Dola Jigme Kalzang is a very fine example of someone acting out of deep compassion as an expression of the Bodhisattva ideal. This ideal – surely the most heroic to which a human being can aspire – takes us a dramatic step beyond the kinds of practice we explored in the last chapter. In the story of the Buddhist wanderers being jeered at in Sāvatthi, we were mainly concerned with patience and forbearance. By breaking the reciprocal relationship between what is received and what is given, one frees oneself from being controlled by outside conditions, particularly by not responding to harm or criticism on the same terms. However, in this chapter we have moved beyond not returning what we are given. Instead we are concerned with taking continuous initiative, with making a positive impact on the world out of active compassion.

This compassion is universal, taking no account of race, gender, age, nationality, or even species. It embraces all life. It is an outward-going force. Jigme Kalzang is quietly walking down the street when he sees something going on which, by any normal human standards, is not his affair. He is a foreign visitor, and the administration of justice in a small Chinese town is no business of his. Yet his heart cannot bear what is to happen. It is as if a living being is about to suffer the fires of hell, and is crying out for someone to come to his aid. So Jigme Kalzang takes the initiative, and intervenes in the only way he can, stealing suffering and death from the thief under false pretences. The man is fortunate indeed that passing by is a Bodhisattva who is prepared to give anything, even his life, to help living beings.

This story has a very strong effect on me. So many of the world's problems and individuals' sufferings are caused by antipathies and hatreds, all based on perceived differences: of race, religion, gender, wealth, and so forth. It is moving to discover someone transcending those barriers, so that he could feel so strongly for a criminal, a stranger of a different race. I also find the sentence being carried out on the thief (who may not even have stolen anything that significant) a horrendous one. An English peer once remarked, 'Men are not hanged for stealing horses, but that horses may not be stolen.'[17] Nonetheless, no amount of stealing could justify the use of the copper horse as a deterrent. Indeed, the torture involved in the execution somehow strikes me with more revulsion than the taking of life. Torture itself, the deliberate and conscious infliction of pain upon another human being, is the absolute antithesis of the Bodhisattva ideal. I am also deeply moved by Jigme Kalzang's selflessness, and uneasily aware that I probably wouldn't have acted in the same way in his position.

It needs to be spelled out that there is nothing martyrish in Jigme Kalzang's action. Unlike some theistic spiritual traditions, Buddhism attaches no special value to dying for your faith. Whilst it naturally sees preparedness to lay down your life for your principles as very positive, virtually no Buddhist would seek out martyrdom. After all, in becoming a martyr, you put some other human being in the position of having to kill you. No Buddhist would want to be the occasion for someone to accumulate the very negative karma associated with killing.

Jigme Kalzang's actions also raise some general issues, some of which we shall examine in the rest of this chapter. We shall be looking at three questions: firstly, what part do compassion and altruism play in the quest for freedom? secondly, how can we work to develop them? and lastly, who was Jigme Kalzang, and how on earth did he come to be capable of such an extraordinary degree of selfless action?

### The Freedom of Compassion

How do compassion and altruism lead us in the direction of freedom? To answer this, we need first to look at what we are trying to free ourselves from. As we saw in the story of Kisā Gotamī, the Buddhist vision is that essentially we are not limited by external circumstances but by the way in which our own consciousness functions. Jigme Kalzang experienced a greater freedom, even when he was bound to the copper horse, than the thief who had just been released from it. The restraints we really need to break are those of our attachment and aversion. To change the image slightly, these emotional forces often drag us along like wild horses in the early part of our lives. Then as we get older and our energy decreases they transform into fear, inertia, and love of comfort to tether us down in one place.

These tendencies to attachment and aversion are based on a fundamental misunderstanding of the nature of things. As we have seen, our unenlightened minds create for us a world of fixed entities, in which we believe ourselves to be a fixed self confronted by other fixed selves and objects. As long as we believe in these seemingly-solid entities we shall interact crudely with other people, like dodgem cars at a fairground – egos bumping into one another, or swerving to avoid perceived threats. The main aim of the Buddhist path is to enable ourselves and others to overcome what some Buddhist texts characterize as these 'primitive beliefs about reality'. Modern-day science has revealed to us a world made up of energy, with everything so fleeting and ephemeral that events cannot be defined in terms of either waves or particles. Although we may know a little about quantum theory, we still use very old-fashioned and crude categories in our everyday thinking about ourselves and our world. In fact, our thinking usually isn't just pre-Einstein and Planck, often it is pre-Copernicus and Galileo. We have not even taken on the idea that the Earth revolves around the Sun; instead we still instinctively feel that everything revolves around us.

How are we to free ourselves from our deeply-held belief in a fixed ego, and the craving which forms a gravitational field around it? The final answer must be through the development of insight into

Reality: seeing with wisdom things as they really are. This is achieved through meditative reflection on such topics as impermanence and the way in which all things arise in dependence upon conditions. These practices will eventually dissolve the illusion of a fixed self, existing in and of itself, surrounded by an 'external world' of inherently-existing people and objects. When we experience the open, constantly transforming, nature of everything, not just as an idea but directly and intuitively, then we shall really become free.

Insight into Reality is achieved (except in the most exceptional individuals) only on the basis of much prior spadework. Until this work has been done we simply have too much emotional investment in our wrong notions of the world to be able or prepared to investigate them deeply. We first have to make the move from self-centredness and self-obsession to generosity, sharing, and concern for others. With this development our ego becomes more expansive and refined. From this state it is more feasible to take the leap of seeing through the ego altogether. Therefore, much of the path to freedom consists in developing concern for others, a kind heart, which empathizes with the sufferings and joys of other people and other forms of life.

This kind-heartedness expresses itself in generosity and ethical action, and generally in sharing in the joys and woes of other beings. Whilst this in itself will not make us free, it certainly will make us far happier, more spontaneous and creative. Through our self-concern we build defensive fortifications, moats and portcullises to protect ourselves, but these in effect become our prisons. Through empathy and generosity we venture beyond the castle walls. Eventually we may enjoy ourselves so much that we even forget to return. Or, from our new vantage point beyond the moat, we may manage to see that the whole great structure was a mirage, providing only an illusion of security.

This altruistic activity leads naturally in the direction of the Bodhisattva ideal. The Bodhisattva path consists of the intensive cultivation of both wisdom and compassion. Through strenuous effort in study, reflection, and meditation one comes to a deep understanding of the true nature of things. Through meditation one also cultivates wholehearted compassion, which one then expresses and reinforces through altruistic actions. Eventually these two great qualities fuse and become inseparable. Deep wisdom sees that the conceptual distinction between oneself and others is not finally true. Then one stands shoulder to shoulder with all life, and compassion becomes no longer something to practise, but rather a natural expression of how one sees the world. One cares for other living beings as naturally as one cares for one's own hands.

### Opening the Heart of Compassion

It is all very well to see that compassion is an essential part of the path to freedom, but how is that deep opening of the heart to be achieved? Firstly, we can encourage ourselves by recognizing that there are situations in which our hearts do open in response to suffering. Perhaps someone close to us succumbs to a painful illness; or we see TV pictures of refugees fleeing from conflict, the victims of a terrorist bomb, or a child hurt in an accident. For a little time at least, our hearts go out to those who are suffering, and we empathize with them as fellow living beings. However, we all too easily lose touch with these feelings, or succumb to so-called 'compassion fatigue'. What we need is a way of sustaining and deepening these responses until they are firmly established, until they become our natural way of responding to life. Over the centuries Buddhism has developed many methods for promoting this emotional opening. As this chapter concerns Tibetan Buddhism, in this section we shall survey some of the methods used to develop compassion in the Tibetan tradition.

In common with most schools of Buddhism, the Tibetan schools use meditation as a principal means for cultivating positive emotion in general. There is a set of four emotions which are fostered in meditation, which form the basis for all positive emotional development. These are known as the 'four immeasurables' because through practice they can be developed to an ever greater extent. The fundamental one, which gives rise to the other three, is loving-kindness, an emotion of friendliness and well-wishing.[18] When this comes into contact with others who are in good states it becomes sympathetic joy – rejoicing that others are happy and creating the causes of future happiness by practising the Dharma. Then when loving-kindness meets with suffering it spontaneously transforms into a feeling of compassion. Naturally, to start with it is easier to develop loving-kindness towards friends and people who treat us well, and harder to develop it towards strangers, and people to whom we feel antipathy. However, the aim of the practice is to go beyond likes and dislikes, and to arrive at an impartial loving-kindness that encompasses all living beings. Thus the fourth of these immeasurables is equanimity.

Whilst these four immeasurables, strongly developed, would in themselves take you a long way towards freedom, Tibetan Buddhism uses further meditations and reflections to awaken the *bodhicitta*, the will to Enlightenment, the deep current of compassion that carries you in the direction of Buddhahood for the sake of all living beings. These were introduced into Tibet by the Indian teacher Atīśa, who crossed the Himalayas in 1042 to help spread the Dharma, despite knowing that the journey would shorten his life.

Atīśa taught two great systems of reflection and meditation for developing the bodhicitta, though it is possible to combine them.[19] The first is known as *lojong*, or mind training. Its central premise, which we have seen before, is that we all act, subtly or crudely, as if our own self was the most important thing in the universe. This self-cherishing, which comes to us naturally, is actually the source of all our woes. Fixated on this self, its needs and desires, its happiness and sorrows, fears and pains, triumphs and disasters, we are never happy. Indeed, the more fixated on it we become, the more constricted our states of mind, and the more we entrap ourselves. Conversely, the more we let go of self-concern and engage ourselves with the rest of life, the more expansive our states of mind and the more fulfilled we become. So the essence of the lojong method is what is called 'exchanging self and other'. One works to overcome self-concern and to put oneself at the service of all life.

There are many reflections and meditations within the lojong tradition to help bring about this very radical reorientation of our being. One very graphic way of familiarizing the mind with this new motivation is known as *tonglen* – 'giving and receiving'. This meditative method involves visualizing that with each in-breath one is taking into oneself all the sufferings and difficulties of other living beings. These are visualized in the form of black smoke. This dissolves in one's heart, where it is transformed by compassion. Then with one's out-breath one sends out happiness and joy to all living beings in the form of brilliant light. This meditation can be a challenging experience. To perform it effectively one needs to have developed the strong conviction that self-cherishing is really a cause of suffering, and that generosity and altruism really are the road to happiness.

The second set of methods stems from the great Indian monk-poet Śāntideva. These involve a series of reflections, beginning with consideration of the sufferings of mundane life. This is not a cold, rational listing of the ills that flesh is heir to, but an empathetic entering into the lives of others, to the point where the extent of suffering in the world becomes so unbearable that one feels motivated to do something about it.

This empathy is strengthened by reflection on our relatedness to other living beings. The Tibetans, along with Buddhist tradition in general, have a strong belief in rebirth. They hold that, because of ignorance of the true nature of things, all living beings have been wandering in states of suffering for endless lifetimes. If this is the case, then during the course of this unthinkable number of lives every living being must have been intimately related to us. At some time, each must have been our friend or sibling, our father or mother. We are asked to reflect particularly on how all living beings have been our mother. Through this reflection the Tibetan tradition aims to draw on the deep feelings of gratitude and love that a child develops in a healthy relationship with its mother, and to expand those feelings to include all beings. (Unfortunately these reflections do not have the desired effect on many Western Buddhists, who at best have a very provisional belief in rebirth, and who sometimes have not had particularly healthy relationships with their parents. In which case it is better to use the tonglen methods described earlier.)

Seeing that all these beings who have been so kind to us over so many lives are trapped in a potentially endless series of lives of suffering, one is then highly motivated to find a way out for them, to follow the way to freedom discovered by the Buddha. Thus, through this series of reflections, repeated day after day, one gradually develops the invincible resolve to become Enlightened in order to help all living beings to free themselves from suffering.

In this section I have talked in terms of systems of meditation and reflection. Although meditation is a very effective tool for emotional transformation, the changes it makes must be carried into action. The Bodhisattva does not wait to become Enlightened before helping others. It is all very good to sit and wish others well, but these positive feelings need to be expressed in acts of generosity and friendliness. Both the systems I have described only function fully and effectively when a 'virtuous circle' is created. This starts with kindling a few sparks of loving-kindness in meditation, and giving expression to it in small acts of kindness and generosity. These help us to feel on more positive terms with ourselves, which makes meditation on friendliness easier, which enables us to give a little more, to be a better friend, and so on. As time goes on, more deeply loving thoughts lead to selfless acts, which create more expansive states of mind. This process culminates in the collapse of all the walls around the heart. Completely freed from thinking in terms of 'me' and 'them', we love and give naturally and spontaneously.

*A Banquet for all Beings*
Who was Dola Jigme Kalzang, who sacrificed his life on the copper horse? Unfortunately we have no written biography of him. We do not even have definite dates for his life, but it must have spanned the latter part of the eighteenth century and the early part of the nineteenth. He was a great meditator and scholar of the Nyingma School – the oldest of the four main schools of Tibetan Buddhism. He lived and taught in eastern Tibet: in Kham and Amdo (regions known for their fine horsemen, though no one ever tamed a more difficult steed than Jigme Kalzang). In the later part of his life he also taught the Dharma in Mongolia.[20]

Although there are relatively few biographical details available, two significant stories about Jigme Kalzang have come down to us. One of them of course is the story of how he met his death while on a visit to China. The other is significant for the insight it provides into what moved him spiritually, and the practices that enabled him to give up his life for a stranger. It concerns a day on which Jigme Kalzang had just begun a three-year solitary meditation retreat in a cave by the Yellow River. Tibetan Buddhism utilizes many meditations involving visualization and mantra recitation. In his retreat Jigme Kalzang was going to spend three years alone, visualizing and reciting the mantra of the tantric deity Vajrakīla. Through visualizing this figure intensively whilst in solitude he aimed to become one with the state of Enlightened freedom that it embodies.

However, on the very first evening of Jigme Kalzang's three-year retreat a wandering yogin happened to shelter in the mouth of his cave. This man began chanting the *Khandrö Kegyang* – a ritual text of the form of practice called Chöd, accompanying himself with a ritual bell and the large, sonorous double-sided drum used in this ritual. Inside his cave, Jigme Kalzang was deeply inspired by the beauty and meaning of the chanting. So the following morning, although he had just vowed to remain in solitude for three years, he broke his retreat and spoke to the yogin, asking what he had been chanting, and from whom he had learned it. The yogin's reply led Jigme Kalzang to forgo his retreat and travel at once to meet Dodrupchen Rimpoche, who became his main teacher, giving him instructions on the Chöd and much else.

What is this Chöd practice that inspired Jigme Kalzang so much? Essentially it is a meditation in which, out of compassion, you imagine offering your physical body for the benefit of all beings. It is a kind of shamanistic sacrifice transmuted into a powerfully effective method for freeing yourself from your deepest attachment. In the course of the Chöd you imagine that your consciousness leaves your physical body, taking the form of a *ḍākinī*. Ḍākinīs are female figures – wild, ecstatic, and naked apart from some ornaments made from human bone. When you encounter any Tibetan meditational figure, whether in art or literature, the main point to realize is that they are all embodiments of states of mind. You have to ask yourself, what state of consciousness is being conveyed through this symbolic figure? Through identifying with the wild, ecstatic and naked ḍākinī, your mind takes on the qualities of freedom, blissful wisdom, and non-attachment. The bone ornaments, among other meanings, symbolize the overcoming of the fear of death.

In this ḍākinī form, you observe your physical body which, consciousness having left it, is now lifeless. With a sharp knife you then cut up the corpse and put the pieces into a gigantic skull cup. From the point of view of your everyday consciousness, which clings to the physical body as its most precious possession, such a procedure might seem an expression of masochism or self-hatred, but for those who are more spiritually developed (and the Chöd is certainly not a practice for beginners), the situation is very different. The cutting up of the corpse is symbolic of using the sharp blade of wisdom to sever wrong concepts about the body. Analysing the physical body into its parts, you nowhere find a self-existent 'I'. Eventually you realize that the body is not 'I' or 'me' or 'mine'.

You see too that at death the elements of the body will return to become part of the elements in the world around you. At death, you will breathe out for the last time, and the air will be absorbed into the surrounding atmosphere. The heat will radiate away into space, and the body will become cold. If you are buried your bones will return to the earth. If you are cremated your blood and so forth will turn to smoke, steam, and ashes. All these elements were only borrowed in the form of the coffee you drank, the cereals and vegetables you ate, the air you breathed in. It is the mind which has turned these temporary meetings of elements into a prized possession to be defended, safeguarded, beautified, photographed, and so much else.

Once the pieces of the body are in the skull cup, they are heated by a fire set blazing beneath it. All the impurities are boiled away, and what is left is nectar, which through the power of mantra is multiplied and increased. This wonderful nectar is then offered out of devotion to a great assembly of Enlightened beings. It is also shared with all living beings, fulfilling their wishes and healing all their suffering.

Thus the practice develops both wisdom and compassion, the two main elements of the Enlightenment experience. Whilst these qualities are developed partly by analytical and reflective meditation, the Chöd takes it for granted that that work has already been done. It aims to enable the meditator to take these qualities even deeper into his or her being. In the course of the ritual one lives out, in vivid imagination, the process of freeing oneself from the body, and making an offering of it with deep compassion for all that lives.

People with no experience of it often feel that meditation is a waste of time, an escapist pursuit that has no effects in the real world. However, nothing could be further from the truth. Meditation is the process of habituating the mind to act in ways which are wise and compassionate. Whilst – in the beginners' stage of meditation – its effects on the rest of one's life may be very short-lived (so that, for instance, one may meditate on compassion, and minutes afterwards find oneself acting in bad-tempered or selfish ways), as one persists one's mind becomes increasingly accustomed to dwelling in the states of mind promoted by the meditation. As our mind leads all our actions – indeed our actions are largely the bodying forth of our mental states – over time meditation transforms the whole manner in which we act in the world.

I can think of no more graphic demonstration of this than the story of Dola Jigme Kalzang. Having been deeply moved by the chanting of the Chöd ritual outside his cave, he himself took it up and practised it. As a result he was transformed by it to such a remarkable extent that, confronted with a complete stranger about to suffer a horrible death, he immediately stepped forward to take on the suffering of that anonymous thief. He placed his own body into the skull cup of the copper horse, and in its fires his body became an offering for the benefit of the thief and of all living beings. Through years of Dharma practice, he had realized the nature of his body and mind, so he could die happily, understanding the nature of birth and death. Through his practice of the Bodhisattva path, his mind had become an ocean of nectar, of great compassion for everything that lives.

# 6

# Do You Understand the Words or the Meaning?

*Tantra and Symbolic Biography*
In this chapter we shall be looking at another story preserved in the Tibetan tradition that has something to teach us about freedom, particularly about how we limit our freedom when we fail to recognize the pitfalls inherent in our use of language, or confuse knowing about the path to freedom with actually following it. This story, though, comes from a much earlier era than that of Dola Jigme Kalzang. We need to move from China to India, and go back a further 800 years to the eleventh century, to see an episode in the life of Nāropa.

Nāropa was the Indian Buddhist teacher of the Tibetan Marpa, who in his turn was the teacher of Milarepa, perhaps the most famous meditator ever produced in Tibet. The lineages of teaching and practice that derive from these great figures are very important for Tibetan Buddhism. As we have seen, the Buddhism of Tibet makes much use of symbolic ritual, visualization, and mantra as ways of freeing the mind from its limiting conditionings. These forms of meditation are laid out in a class of Buddhist texts called *tantras*. Nāropa is acknowledged as one of the eighty-four *mahāsiddhas* – a group of great sages who gained the freedom of Enlightenment through practising tantric meditation. Reflecting this, the biographies of tantric teachers are full of images and symbols. These tantric life stories often conflate descriptions of their subjects' outer and inner lives, so that symbols and images are superimposed on outer reality. This makes it hard at times to tell whether they are describing historical events or processes of inner development. This may well reflect the experience of the tantric sages themselves, whose symbolic meditation often profoundly affected their perception of what we think of as the everyday world. The incident we shall be looking at in this chapter, which transforms Nāropa's life almost within minutes, has this dreamlike or visionary quality. It is an irruption of a higher reality into the everyday world.

### A Scholar's Life is Turned Upside-Down by an Old Woman

Nāropa was born the son of a royal family. Even as a young child he was deeply drawn to the Dharma, and he spent part of his youth studying with Buddhist teachers in Kashmir. Then he returned to his kingdom and, following his parents' wishes, was married to a young Buddhist woman. However, after a while the couple decided to separate in order to continue their practice of the Dharma independently. From then on Nāropa devoted himself to his Buddhist studies.

Eventually he came to Nālandā, in present-day Bihar, which was the greatest Buddhist university of its day. At its height it had ten thousand monks, and there were hundreds of teachers giving talks on the Dharma every day. Nālandā was like a large monastic city, and at each of its gates there was a 'professor' who taught a particular speciality in the Dharma. At that time the post at the north gate was vacant, so a great debate was held to find the best person to fill it. Nāropa (who at this stage in his life was known as Abhayakīrti – 'Famed for Fearlessness') defeated all the other candidates, and took up the post.

To celebrate his appointment the scholars at Nālandā invited some Hindu teachers to come for a debate in front of the King. The terms were that the losers, with all their followers, would convert to the winners' point of view. By this stage in its history Buddhism had developed the arts of debate and logical argument to a very high degree. Abhayakīrti took the leading part in the debate, and the Hindus were all vanquished and had to convert to the Dharma. Then Abhayakīrti sang a song of pleasure at the victory of the Dharma:

> With the iron hook of grammar, the lore of knowledge, logic
> And spiritual precepts,
> I, the Elder Abhayakīrti,

*Have scattered the opponents as a flock of sparrows.*
*With the axe of grammar, the lore of knowledge, logic*
*And spiritual precepts*
*I have felled the opponents' tree.*
*With the lamp of certainty in logic and precepts,*
*I have burnt the darkness of my foes' ignorance.*
*With the sacred jewels of the three disciplines*
*Have I removed the dirt of impurity.*
*With instruction's battering ram*
*Have I conquered the vicious city of bewilderment.*
*At Nālandā in the presence of the king*
*Have I felled the ever trembling tree of the heretics.*
*With the razor of the Buddha's doctrine*
*I have shaved the hair of my opponent heretics,*
*And have raised the banner of the Buddha's doctrine.*[21]

He had good reason to be pleased with what had happened, but one can hear a tinge of personal pride in his achievement, which is not all that healthy.

Nāropa's star steadily rose at Nālandā, until finally he became abbot, and was acknowledged as the greatest Buddhist scholar of his age. It was eight years after that debate, at the height of his fame, that an event took place which was to transform his life.

We find him in his study, surrounded by piles of books. It is a fine morning, with the sunlight streaming in, but he is seated poring over his texts, with his back to the sun. He is immersed in grammar, logic, and other subjects when suddenly a terrifying shadow falls across the pages. Looking round, he sees an old woman, who seems to have appeared from nowhere. She is a gruesome sight, having thirty-seven 'ugly features'. The text tells us

> Her eyes were red and deep-hollowed; her hair was fox-coloured
> and dishevelled; her forehead large and protruding; her face had
> many wrinkles and was shrivelled up; her ears were long and
> lumpy; her nose was twisted and inflamed; she had a yellow beard
> streaked with white; her mouth was distorted and gaping; her
> teeth were turned in and decayed; her tongue made chewing
> movements and moistened her lips; she made sucking noises and
> licked her lips; she whistled when she yawned; she was weeping
> and tears ran down her cheeks; she was shivering and panting for

breath; her complexion was darkish blue; her skin rough and thick; her body bent and askew; her neck curved; she was hump-backed; and, being lame, she supported herself on a stick.[22]

She asks Nāropa, 'What are you looking into?'

Nāropa replies, 'I'm reading books on grammar, logic, and monastic discipline.' Then the old hag asks him, 'Do you understand the words of the Dharma texts you read, or the meaning?' and he replies 'I understand the words,' at which she looks delighted and starts dancing round the room, waving her stick in the air and laughing to herself. Nāropa is taken aback, but is pleased to have made this strange old creature so happy. Thinking that he will make her even happier, he adds, 'I also understand the meaning.'

At this the old woman completely changes. She looks crestfallen, starts sadly wandering around the room, and throws her stick on the ground. Nāropa is confused, he cannot understand what is going on, so he says, 'Why were you so pleased when I said I understood the words, and yet so sad when I said I understood the meaning?' And the old woman responds, 'I was happy that you, a great scholar, didn't lie, but openly admitted that you understood the words and not the meaning.' Now Nāropa is really taken aback, because if *he* – the abbot of Nālandā, who has studied the Dharma ever since he was eight years old – doesn't understand it, who on earth does? He bursts out, '*Who* then understands the meaning?' To which the old woman slyly replies, 'My brother!'

And with that she disappears like a rainbow into the sky.

This extraordinary episode precipitates an enormous upheaval in Nāropa's being, a complete reversal of his previous view of himself. He realizes straightaway, intuitively, that all his knowledge of the Dharma is not enough. At the same time he has a very deep insight into the unsatisfactory nature of conditioned existence. He resolves on the spot to stop being abbot of Nālandā and 'go forth' – to go in search of a teacher who understands the meaning – someone whose life and being are expressions of the Dharma.

Naturally he is begged to stay by all the 10,000 monks at Nālandā, and by all the other teachers. But he is quite convinced, after his meeting with the strange old woman, that he is wasting his time as a dealer in ideas, however subtle and profound, if he himself does not embody them. He refuses to change his mind and leaves

Nālandā. After many difficulties he eventually finds the old woman's brother, who is called Tilopa. Tilopa becomes his teacher, and after even more difficulties Nāropa finally discovers the limitless freedom of Enlightenment.

### The Dharma as a Raft to Freedom

What can we learn from this story that can help us in our quest for freedom? What is the old woman trying to point out to Nāropa? The question she confronts Nāropa with, that she confronts *us* with, is 'Do you understand the words, or the meaning?' This raises a number of very relevant issues for anyone trying to use the Dharma to transform their lives; in fact for any human being.

In order to understand the Dharma, we need to have the right motivation. We can engage with it as an intellectual pursuit, as some scholars do in depth, but unless we recognize that the Dharma is intended to help us to develop as human beings, to find our freedom and become Enlightened, then we do not really understand it. It is not that we understand it to some degree. However much we may know about Buddhism, unless we are trying to follow it as a path to freedom we do not understand the Dharma at all. We have totally misapprehended it, like someone trying to use a guitar as a frying-pan. This is the first point that comes out of the old woman's question: we need to have the right motivation, otherwise we can know all the words but we shall not grasp the meaning at all. If the Dharma is not taking us towards Enlightenment, if we are not using it to guide us along the path to freedom, then it is not the Dharma for us.

Secondly, her question relates to a simile once used by the Buddha. He said that the Dharma is like a raft which we can use to carry us across from the shore of suffering and unsatisfactoriness to the shore of freedom. Having arrived at the 'further shore' we can leave all these verbal teachings behind. Thus the Dharma is progressive, and its forms, which are means to an end, finally have to be transcended. Therefore we need to be wary of becoming too caught up in written formulations. Words are very useful as pointers, but we have to see them in a suggestive, almost poetic, sense. The Buddha said that the truth, the Dharma, is *atakkāvacara*, which means 'beyond the realm of rational thought'. So we should not expect to catch the ultimate truth in the 'iron net of logic', and we need to beware of becoming bogged down in words. Rather, we should use them lightly, as springboards to launch ourselves towards the truth.

Another consideration that arises from this simile of the raft is that we may not need to study all that much written Dharma. It is essential that people learn the essentials of the Dharma, and clarify their understanding of it. I am very much in favour of some people making a deep study of Buddhism. However, there is always a danger of becoming lost in study as an end in itself. Just as most of us accumulate more possessions than we really need, so we accumulate ideas about Buddhism that we cannot really use. The comparison of the Dharma with a raft suggests that we do not usually need all that much theory. After all, a raft is a very basic method of transport. All you require are a few planks tied together to keep you afloat, and perhaps some kind of sail. Similarly, to practise the Dharma all you need are a few planks, such as the Refuges and Precepts, the Four Noble Truths, some simple methods of meditation, and perhaps some kind of devotional exercise for a sail.

The important thing is to start, to commit yourself to the journey and cast off. You must then learn how to handle your raft, get to know its every trick in the difficult winds of saṁsāra. After that, once you have had some practical experience, and perhaps been washed overboard once or twice, you will evaluate each new teaching with the practical eye of the lone seaman whose very life may depend on the decision; 'Does it help me to sail faster? Does it really serve some useful function, or will it merely burden down the raft, making it sink lower in the water?' If we view Buddhist teachings in this practical, critical way, we shall avoid the mirage of mistaking theory for practice. So often, instead of putting together and actually launching simple rafts, we build quinqueremes and galleons in our imagination. Or we construct opulent gin-palace paddle steamers out of all the schools of Buddhism, and try to enlist learned men as crew to do our crossing for us. Then we recline on the sun deck, reading advanced teachings like travel brochures, and are lulled into thinking that we are really moving, while all the time we remain firmly anchored to suffering.[23]

### The Pitfalls of Language

So far the old woman's question has provoked three ideas. Firstly, we do not necessarily comprehend the meaning of the Dharma just because we know the concepts. We only begin to understand the Dharma if we use it for the purpose for which it was intended: to help us to develop in the direction of freedom. Secondly, as the Dharma is a raft, we have to see it in a progressive, poetic way, using words as springboards towards truth. And thirdly, we do not need to accumulate knowledge for its own sake; we require only whatever helps us to keep moving along the path to freedom. But there is a great deal more in the old woman's question about words and meanings than that.

We are using language almost all the time we are awake. We spend years of our lives talking. We may spend years more reading, and being talked to by television, radio, and films. When there is no one else around we keep on talking to ourselves, chattering away in the privacy of our own mind.

Language is the magic which we use to control our world. Primitive human beings, faced by 'nameless dread', slowly began using language to describe their environment. At that time, the use of words and symbols became essential to magic. If you knew the name of something, that word stood in place of the animal, the natural force, etc. that it denominated, and through the use of words you could gain power over the objects to which they referred. This magic of language has developed over the millennia and forms the basic tool of science and technology, through which we have gained power over the environment to an unprecedented degree.

In our everyday lives too, as we have seen, we resort to this word-magic from morning to night. But if we want to progress spiritually, to become truly free, then we need to understand that there are certain pitfalls in using language. There are ways in which words do not accord with reality. Especially there are certain dangers in conceptual thinking. If we do not recognize these dangers then sooner or later our progress on the path to freedom will be blocked. So it is time to examine more closely this word-magic that we all conjure with so well and so easily, that we use continuously and often take for granted.

What are these pitfalls that are inherent in language? Talking about them is complicated by the fact that we have to use words to describe the limitations of words. I shall discuss them under four headings, but in essence they all come down to one danger: the tendency to take words as real and to lose touch with our actual experience. The four pitfalls that we are going to look at are (1) bending our experience to conform to our language, (2) creating false entities – treating abstractions as things, (3) covering our experience in sticky labels, (4) taking life for granted by treating descriptions as explanations.

### 1. Bending our Experience to Conform to our Language

If we live all the time in the sphere of words, it is possible to lose touch with our experience. Then what often happens is that we start to bend our experience into line with our ideas. Reality is incredibly rich and multidimensional. In every moment there is an inconceivable amount to experience. By comparison, conceptual thought is puny. In a sense it is two-dimensional. It marches in straight lines from left to right (or in other directions, as with Arabic or Mandarin) across the page. Clearly, in order to describe the world to ourselves, we need to use language. Ideally there should be a spiralling dialogue between our experience and our description of it. Experiencing life as deeply as we can, we should hone our language into as wieldy a tool as possible for describing it. This refinement of our conceptual description will then allow us to dive more deeply into our experience. The continuing effort to explore experience and refine our picture of it will free us from false and inadequate ideas about the nature of life and how we exist, and enable us to experience ever more fully.

Unfortunately, what often happens if we are not careful is that, rather than widening our capacity to use language so that it expresses our experience more adequately, we narrow down our experience so that it conforms to our limited views about life. Then, without realizing what we are doing, we may assume that we have caught all of this fantastically rich experience, this multidimensional reality, in our two-dimensional concepts. It is like taking a baby elephant and trying to squeeze it into a large suitcase. Try as we might we can never fit it all in. Even if we sit on it, the ears stick out, the tail won't go, or we don't know what to do with the trunk. At this point we should realize that the suitcase will never be big enough, and either begin building a much bigger container, or forget the whole project and let the elephant roam free. However, it is easy to start ignoring aspects of experience that don't fit, and to discard them. Then we are left with a neat, tidy suitcase with only a small part of the elephant inside.

We have solved our problem. The suitcase of our concepts is firmly closed to new ways of looking at the world. As far as we are concerned, life is just those parts in our case. Nothing outside exists. Unfortunately, apart from impoverishing our experience, acting in this way also leaves us feeling uneasy and insecure. From time to time we shall hear sounds of trumpeting and stamping coming from some part of life which we now refuse to acknowledge. These scare us, and we may respond by holding even more tightly to our narrowly circumscribed concepts. Thus we end up imprisoned in a closed world of ideas, shut off from any experience that is not in accord with them. We have created a world in which we feel secure but somehow rather dead. We feel dissatisfied, but the whole process may have happened largely unconsciously, so we may not understand how we came to lose our freedom.

A very basic example of this is the way in which language divides up everything into subject and object. According to the Dharma, reality doesn't work in terms of subject and object. But our language does, so that is how we experience the world. From the time we first begin to understand language we are not just teaching ourselves to speak, we are learning to see the world in a particular way. So this is the danger: rather than experiencing our experience, feeling our feelings, seeing what we see, we bend, twist, and narrow everything down to fit into what we can conceptualize, what we can think, the words that we have.

In this regard, it is a valuable experience to learn a second language, because it makes us more aware. There are things we can say in one language that we cannot say adequately or in quite the same way in another. That makes us question the language, it throws us back on our actual experience: what do I actually feel, what is it that I am really trying to get across? This, then, is the first danger, bending our experience to conform to our language.

### 2. Creating False Entities – Treating Abstractions as Things
This is what is technically known as reifying concepts. *Res* in Latin means a thing. We take an abstraction and treat it as if it was something real and solid that we could get hold of. We all use words to make abstractions from our experience, which is a useful and necessary activity. But the danger is that we may then separate that abstraction from the experience to which it relates. In particular we

need to beware of jumping from specifics to generalizations. If I once have a difficult experience with some Dutch people, I have to be careful that I do not start saying 'The Dutch are difficult.' I would then have expanded my experience of half a dozen people to include over 14,000,000 human beings. All too often we take some small experience, expand it by generalization in this way, and then develop unjustified feelings and opinions about those abstractions. To the extent that we do this we shall have lost touch with reality.

Abstraction involves a process of extracting common qualities from specific examples. However, once we have made, or learned, an abstraction we have to be careful that it does not lose touch with its moorings in actual experience. We never have peace separate from peaceful people; we never meet Enlightenment separate from an Enlightened person. But in words we can.

Abstraction misused can also lead to a tendency to want a title or some credential without the experience to which it should refer. For instance, some years ago I read a book describing the experiences of a Westerner going to Japan to study karate.[24] After he had been attending classes at a karate school in Tokyo for two or three weeks, he naïvely asked one of his instructors, 'How long will it take me to get a black belt?' The teacher was really offended. He opened a drawer, pulled out a black belt, said, 'You want a black belt? There!' and threw it at him, saying 'Now get out.' Some Westerners imagine the status they would have if they had a black belt around their waists. The Japanese don't think in those terms, they think of training and working to the level where you are a first *dan*, where you have reached that degree of skill, speed, and strength, but because we can separate the label from the experience, we can think in terms of getting a black belt.

So while abstractions are useful tools for thinking about the world, we need to handle them with care and not take them for granted. When we find ourselves using abstractions and generalizations we have constantly to refer them back to our experience, to the actual basis in reality from which we are producing that abstraction. What is the raw material in our own perceptions – in what we actually see, feel, etc. – from which we have derived this abstract idea? Where we have abstract ideals, too, it is important that we relate them to our current experience. What can we concretely do, here and now, to move closer to embodying our ideals?

### 3. *Covering our Experience in Sticky Labels*

To understand this we need to see that our first use of words is as a labelling process. All the time, every second as we sit reading, we are being bombarded by impressions through all our senses, a great confused mass of them. The first thing that happens as they come in is that they are ordered, structured, and identified – they are labelled. The aspect of our consciousness that structures our experience in this way is technically called *saṁjñā* in Sanskrit. This labelling process which is going on all the time is very useful and necessary. But there is a danger. We can substitute the labels for reality. It is as if our interest stops at the point at which we have successfully produced a label.

During the 1980s I regularly led Buddhist retreats in Tuscany. At the end of each three-month retreat I would go to Florence to visit the Uffizi, one of the world's greatest art galleries. I used to find it very interesting to watch other visitors going round the gallery. Many local people went, and would often spend a long time absorbed in looking at one or two pictures. There was also a steady stream of tourists from around the world. Most of the tourists, on entering a room full of amazing paintings, would immediately go up close to one to read the artist's name. If the painting was by someone famous, such as Botticelli or Raphael, they would stand and look at it for maybe fifteen or twenty seconds. If it was by someone of whom they had never heard, they would glance cursorily at it, before going off to look at the next name.

There is a serious danger that we shall learn to stop our experience at the point where we have a label for things. Eventually, we end up living in a world of sticky labels, plastering them all over our experience. From my window I can see into a neighbouring garden. At a certain point, from the mass of sense-impressions, I may identify the figure of a woman. My brain does a quick comparison with similar stored images from the past and I think 'Oh, it's Ann,' and return to my writing. 'Ann' is the most general of the various labels that I can put on this experience: neighbour, doctor, generous friend, etc. None of these labels begins to do justice to the reality of this human being, with her complex life experience.

However, absorbed in my writing, I may not see the unique, rich experience in front of me. Lost in a world of sticky labels I can see hardly anything. I just think 'Oh, there's Ann.' It is as if we were to move from a world of unique, constantly changing flesh and blood human beings and replace it with a world of recognition-symbols where people have become like the stick figures representing men and women on toilet doors. We have to make a real effort to come back to our experience, to go beyond the labels, to start seeing what is there again, to come back into our senses, back into our feelings, rather than taking everything for granted.

Nouns in this way are worse than verbs. A noun is something unchanging, static; like a name it just stays there. Verbs at least denote action, there is some kind of movement. They come closer to the Buddhist view of life as constant change. It is interesting that those poets considered the greatest in English, like Shakespeare, turn out to be the ones who use the highest proportion of verbs in their language. It would remind us more of reality if we could think of a flower as a 'flowering', or even if I could think of my neighbour as an 'Ann-ing', so there was a sense of movement and of life. Otherwise – because I use the same label, Ann, each time I see her – I may take her for granted, and make the mistake of thinking that she is the same as the last time I saw her. Thus we need to be careful that we do not stop at the point of recognition, which is very easy to do, and that we recognize the change and the uniqueness behind the un-changing labels. Otherwise life becomes very dull and lifeless, with the same old labels for the same old things – which are not really the same old things at all. Ever.

Part of the difficulty is that labels are very convenient. They can be tossed about carelessly, when they become jargon. Even in Buddhist circles it is easy to have plenty of jargon; each group has certain phrases and ways of teaching which are much used. Newcomers wishing to join the group often pick up these phrases and use them to parade their allegiance to it, often without fully understanding them or being able to recognize the experiences to which they refer. More long-standing members may find the phrases rolling off their tongues habitually without making any feeling connection with the spiritual experiences that they describe. But frequently, because we all recognize the phrases, even when they are used without under-standing or feeling, everybody nods wisely.

## 4. Treating Descriptions as Explanations

There are more implications to our use of language to label our experience. We usually take the world for granted at a deep level, because we take our capacity to label – our description – as if it was an explanation. To illustrate this, I would like you to try something for a minute. Gently close your eyes and conjure up in your mind's eye the image of a rose, a beautiful red rose. It can have as few or as many petals as you like. See it as clearly as you can. If you like you can also allow yourself to smell its perfume. Allow the image to dissolve away, then slowly open your eyes.

You may not have been able to visualize very clearly, your image of the rose may not have been all that sharp, but you could probably attempt the exercise quite happily. However, the fact is that you do not know what you did. If I were to ask you, you might say, 'I did what you asked. I imagined a red rose.' If I were to push you to explain a bit further you might say 'Well, I conjured it up in my mind's eye.' But where did that rose come from? When you dissolved it away where did it go? In what space did you visualize it?

The real problem with words is that they enable us to take life for granted. Because we can label and describe things, we think we have explained them. But our 'explanations' are often only descriptions that make us feel emotionally secure. We have words, a common set of tokens to pass around to say 'I imagined a red rose,' but when we explore that experience we find it is inconceivable. We do not really know what happened.

We live in a magical world which, most of the time, we can describe to ourselves sufficiently well to feel secure – unconcerned that we cannot really explain what is going on. We accept that description as if it were really an explanation. But the whole of life is inconceivable. Our experience is ungraspable. If we could really experience the fact that our concepts have nothing to do with the ultimate nature of things, then straight away we should become a Stream-entrant, irreversibly bound for Enlightenment. We would have entered the mysterious gateway to Reality called the *animitta samādhi* – the concentration on signlessness.

At this point you may be wondering about the nature of wisdom in Buddhism. Is that not an explanation of the nature of life and death? When we finally see things as they are, isn't everything explained? As I understand it, when we come to the end of the path to freedom we are still left (thankfully) with the inconceivable, the ungraspable. We are still in this magical universe. At the end of the path we do not discover the answer, the rational formula that deals with all our questions. Rather we come to an intuitive understanding, an experience so fulfilling that it takes away all our questions. Wisdom consists in diving directly and deeply into our experience; swimming about in it so contentedly that it never even occurs to us to ask 'What is it for?'

### The True Nature of the Old Woman

Having seen some of the dangers inherent in words, perhaps it would be better to work more with symbols, because symbols tend not to get so fixed, they do not go so hard and lumpy and dead on us. They have a numinous quality that speaks to us of a world beyond themselves. So this seems an opportune point at which to return to Nālandā, and Nāropa's meeting with the old woman, and see into what kind of world their symbolic encounter leads us.

We first saw Nāropa poring over his books with his back to the sun. Symbolically, he has become lost in words, and is no longer using Buddhism as a path to the sun of Enlightenment. When the old woman appears he probably instinctively labels her: 'It's an old woman.' However, this label is totally inadequate to describe what he is faced with. He is in for a shock that will jolt him out of the world of labels back into the world of experience.

Who is this old woman? Well, *The Life and Teaching of Nāropa* actually tells us: it says that she is the ḍākinī Vajrayoginī. In the last chapter, we saw that the practitioner of the Chöd ritual visualizes himself or herself as a ḍākinī. Ḍākinīs symbolize the freedom and inspiration that spring from the realization of the emptiness of all phenomena. This open quality to all our experience is symbolized in the tantra by blue sky. The Tibetans translate the Sanskrit *ḍākinī* as *khandroma*, which means something like 'female sky-goer'. So the ḍākinīs play and delight in the blue sky of emptiness. They are usually represented in Tantric Buddhism as brilliantly coloured, naked, dancing female figures. As well as being symbols of liberated consciousness, they frequently appear as the heralds or communicators of higher states of consciousness. They represent the irruption of states of spiritual inspiration into everyday consciousness, so in *Meeting the Buddhas* I called them the muses of the Transcendental.[25]

'Ḍākinī' can also describe a spiritual friend, a human being who has ḍākinī-like qualities, and who fires you and inspires you to follow the path to freedom. But here the old woman clearly represents an inner experience. After all his years studying the Dharma, all of a sudden something comes alive in Nāropa which at last takes him beyond words, which changes his whole life, affecting him so powerfully that he leaves everything behind. His old views are broken up, and he comes into contact with a higher faculty in himself that perceives reality through images and symbols. In fact the old woman's very appearance is symbolic, with those thirty-seven ugly features. For Buddhists this number is charged with special associations, as it recalls a set of positive states or qualities known as the thirty-seven aids to Enlightenment (Sanskrit, *bodhipakṣya-dharmāḥ*). After the ḍākinī has disappeared like a rainbow into the sky, Nāropa sings a song expressing his realization of the unsatisfactoriness of mundane life. This song too has thirty-seven images. Here are a few of them:

> 'Tis like a deer chasing a mirage....
> It is a fragile water-plant,
> The intangible reflection of the moon in water,
> A bubble of bewilderment,
> Fleeting mist and rippling water,
> A snake conquering by touch and sight,
> The taste of honey on a razor blade,...[26]

*A Doctrine Follower in the Hall of Mirrors*
We have seen that here the ḍākinī represents a higher imaginative faculty bursting into life. But why does she appear as ugly? Ḍākinīs are usually beautiful young dancing figures. To Nāropa she appears not as a young girl but as an old hag. There are two reasons she might adopt this ghastly form.

Nāropa has been a very strong example of the type of character known as a 'doctrine follower' in Buddhism. Doctrine followers are personalities of an intellectual tendency whose predominant negative emotion is hatred or aversion. They tend to move towards freedom by penetrating into the faults of ordinary life, going deeper and deeper into why it is unsatisfactory. If you succeed in this approach to the Dharma, then by seeing through saṁsāra and releasing your attachment to it, you finally arrive at an experience of the permanent fulfilment of Nirvāṇa, or Enlightenment. So perhaps the ḍākinī appears ugly here because she represents the outcome of the path that Nāropa has followed. He has approached Reality by reflecting on the faults of the mundane: how compared with the beauty and total satisfaction of Enlightenment, ordinary life is ugly and unful-filling. Thus the ḍākinī appears with thirty-seven ugly features, and Nāropa's mind is filled with images of saṁsāra's dangers.

Though this is the immediate outcome of his encounter with the ḍākinī, very quickly the effects of their meeting take Nāropa on to a radically different, though equally effective, track. He is totally changed, and becomes a 'faith follower'. He gives up all his books and devotes himself wholeheartedly to seeking his guru Tilopa, relying entirely on devotion and meditation.

There is another possible explanation (less flattering for Nāropa) for the ḍākinī's ugly appearance. As abbot of Nālandā he has become very successful in his 'Buddhist career', and his reading with his back to the sun could suggest that he has settled down and lost his sense of the Dharma as a path to freedom. Perhaps he has reached a point where he does not welcome the next stage in his spiritual develop-ment. When it appears, in the form of Vajrayoginī, he cannot joyfully embrace it, he sees it as unattractive. If we take a ḍākinī for granted, if we do not welcome her, she becomes old and ugly for us.

There is always a risk that our practice of the Dharma will become comfortable and self-satisfied. Perhaps we have made a strong effort in the past. Maybe when we first found the Dharma we were not very happy, so we were very motivated to throw ourselves into meditation and other practices. After a while, as a result of our efforts, we started to feel more content. However, this meant that our initial motivation disappeared. We may have settled down on a plateau, or at least what we hope is a plateau, of reasonable happi-ness. Also, there is always the very human tendency to give in to other people's views of ourselves. If we make some spiritual pro-gress, our friends may start telling us how good we are, as all the scholars at Nālandā praised Nāropa for his great scholarship. As a result, we may start thinking that we need not make much further effort.

When I was a child, one of the fairground attractions was the Hall of Mirrors. You would go into a large booth, and down both sides would be mirror after mirror. All the mirrors were made in a different way, so that in the first you might have a huge head and a tiny body, in the second you could be squat and dwarf-like. In the third one you might look about three inches wide and fifteen feet tall, and so on. All the time we are being presented with other people's views of ourselves, all of them different, and in a way this is like living in a Hall of Mirrors. We have our own mirror in which we preen ourselves to see how good we look. Other people also hold up mirrors to us. We stand in front of some and they do not show us in a very good light, so we hastily move on. Eventually maybe we find one that shows us as we like to imagine ourselves, and we remain motionless in front of it.

### Breaking the Mirrors

This could be Nāropa, it could be us: settled down in the spiritual life, preening ourselves in the mirrors of our own self-image and those of our friends who reflect us in the way we want to see ourselves. Then along comes the ḍākinī, and her influence shatters our cosy world. The ḍākinī may be our spiritual friend – someone who sees that we have settled down, and gently and skilfully gives us a prod. The ḍākinī may be the stirrings of our imagination, or the ḍākinī may be an upsurge of what we might call spiritual impatience, from a deeper level of our being. We may have been strolling gently along in the spiritual life, perhaps for years, making some progress, occasional efforts, occasional lapses, then one day a strange mood creeps over us. We have a sense of positive frustration and impatience. Suddenly, we feel tired of lukewarm practice, of being half-hearted about the Dharma. We feel sick of three steps forward and two steps back. Something in us *really* wants to do this, to get somewhere with our spiritual life, to win our freedom, and nothing is going to stand in our way.

We may have gone along to yet another meditation class at our local Buddhist centre; we may have been reading yet another Dharma book, perhaps even *The Life and Teaching of Nāropa*, but all of a sudden, in that moment, something happens. Impatience and a sense of urgency combine and a kind of explosion takes place in our heart. It is an explosion that carries away our old entrenched self. It may even for a few moments carry away our physical body. We find ourselves on a new plane, in a new realm. And as we find ourselves there, within our heart, on a red lotus, there leaps up a wild ecstatic female figure, a ḍākinī. And she is dancing, her feet trampling on a figure embodying all our fear and laziness, half-heartedness, and dullness. In her right hand she brandishes a chopper which cuts through everything that ties us to suffering. Its handle is a *vajra*, a tantric symbol that unites all the qualities of a diamond and a thunderbolt. In her left hand she holds a cup made from a human skull from which she drinks the blissful nectar of knowledge of the insubstantial nature of all things. She wears a necklace of the skulls of all our wrong views. She is red, naked, with dishevelled hair, for she is too much in love with freedom to care about how she looks.' She has a halo of wisdom flames that burn up all our tendencies to become snared by language, all our inadequate concepts about reality. And she spins in our heart, and dances.

The dancing red figure is fascinating and compelling. So it is a shock when, turning our gaze outwards again for a moment, we see a wall of glass, with the dancing image endlessly distorted, twisted in a labyrinth of reflections, from one mirror to the next to the next. But the ḍākinī is not confused, she holds to her own experience. She feels directly the vajra chopper in her right hand, and as she spins in her freedom-dance, sending out endless replicas of herself, these emanations smash all the mirrors, sending fragments of glass flying in all directions. The shards of the broken prison of mirrors fly outwards to reveal a vast blue sky, the blue sky of infinite freedom.

But in the mind of the ḍākinī the word 'infinite' does not arise. In the mind of the ḍākinī, the word 'freedom' does not arise. In the mind of the ḍākinī, no words and concepts arise.

She is far too busy dancing.

# 7

## Who Have You Got to Lose?

*The Lion's Roar of Freedom*
Imagine that one evening a friend of yours arrives late for a meeting at your house. He tells you why he was late: a lion has escaped from a lorry in which it was being transported, and is reported to be roaming your neighbourhood. This story would probably have a strong effect on you (unless your friend is the sort of person who tells tales). You would watch quite carefully how you went from your house to the car. You might even decide that it was safer not to leave the house until the lion had been caught. The knowledge that there was a lion on the loose in your neighbourhood would affect your feelings, your imagination. In your mind's eye you would see the beast prowling in the darkness. But if, as your friend was speaking, all of a sudden from outside there came a deep roar, right from the lion's empty belly, something much more profound would happen to you. It would take your breath away. For a moment you would hardly be able to think. You would experience a tremendous kind of thrill, a shock of emotion. It would go right to the pit of your stomach. It would cause the hairs all over your skin to stand on end. That great sound would affect you totally.

I am using this illustration because the Buddha's communication of the freedom of Enlightenment, his teaching of the Dharma, is known in Sanskrit as his *siṁhanāda* – his lion's roar. This term should warn us against thinking that the Buddha's main communication – or, worse still, his only communication – is through words. After all, a lion's roar is not conceptual; it has no intelligible meaning whatsoever. A lion does not stand there and say 'I am a lion and I am going to eat you up.' It just makes a shattering noise which communicates powerfully and directly to everyone and every animal that hears it.

The Dharma includes all attempts by someone who is Enlightened – by an Enlightened mind – to communicate with someone who is as yet unenlightened. In the last chapter we saw some of the many pitfalls of language. Thankfully, the communication of Enlightenment does not only happen on the level of words. Traditionally, there are three levels on which the Dharma can be communicated, three levels on which a Lion of the Dharma can roar. By being aware of the possibility of communication on all three levels we can shake off the shackles of our tendency to focus on language, and become more open to other modes of experience.

The first of these three levels is known as the 'mind transmission of the Jinas'. 'Jina' means 'Conqueror', and is an epithet of the Buddhas, the fully Enlightened ones, who have conquered ignorance and suffering. This mind transmission is telepathic. If you communicate with the Buddha and you are almost on the threshold of Enlightenment yourself, if you are really receptive, then it is as if there is a spark that flashes straight from mind to mind. All of a sudden you know, you understand. This telepathic transmission, this mind transmission of the Jinas, is the highest form of communication of a Buddha.

Secondly we have what is called the 'sign transmission of the Vidyādharas'. The Vidyādharas are the great tantric teachers and practitioners. These great tantric teachers who practise tantric meditation, visualization, and mantras, communicate the Dharma through what they do, and especially through symbolic ritual and gesture. They do not explain the truth to you, they demonstrate it through action. If you are receptive, if you have built up a relationship with them over the years you catch it. You understand what they are pointing out to you.

Thirdly and lastly we have what is termed the 'word transmission of the Ācāryas'. The Ācāryas are ordinary human teachers, who transmit the Dharma mainly by using words and concepts.

These three – the mind transmission of the Jinas, the sign transmission of the Vidyādharas, and the word transmission of the Ācāryas – are actually a hierarchy. The first is higher than the second which is higher that the third. The lower the level of the transmission, the less direct is the communication of the experience of Enlightenment, and therefore the greater also is the possibility of misunderstanding.

The higher levels are always fresh. A telepathic transmission is direct; it flashes straight to you. Communication through deeds, through actions, is always fresh. But words can become sullied, or change their meaning over a period of time. Unfortunately, sometimes words which were fresh, which communicated freedom to someone in the past, may not always work for us now. On hearing them they do not sound like the roars of powerful young lions, but like the echoes of the roar of a rather toothless old lion, or even a stuffed and moth-eaten one.

We tend to think of the Buddha teaching mainly in words and concepts. But if we are aware of these three levels of communication we see that the Buddha only used words and concepts as a last resort, when the person he was trying to communicate with was too obtuse or befuddled for him to be able to get through on a better or higher level. To put it paradoxically, we could say that the Buddha knew that the most direct communication, the loudest roar of all, was a silent roar.

It is worth looking at our own communication in the light of this. Even in everyday interactions it is very easy to put too much weight on what is said, and not to take into account other levels of communication – the way in which people move, how they look, the clothes they wear. Sometimes you can pick up very subtle feelings and impressions from others that verge on being telepathic. All these levels of communication are very valuable. However, all too often we fix our attention on words, and in doing so we miss a great deal of one another's communication.

### A Tantric Meeting

In the story for this chapter we shall move up from the level of words to look at an example of the second level – the sign transmission of the Vidyādharas. In Buddhism there is a healthy tradition of teachings on this level, teachings that have no conceptual content at all. In the Zen Buddhist tradition, you will find many examples of teaching through actions – through blows or gestures or sometimes even through a kind of roar. Some Zen teachers, such as Rinzai, were renowned for the great shouts they gave. There is a story of a disciple who went to a certain Zen master to ask for a teaching and was answered with a shout that left him deaf for three days. In the Tantra, too, we find that teaching is often effected by signs or by actions rather than by words. In this chapter we are going to be concerned with a magnificent example of this direct communication through action by an outstanding tantric teacher. In order to hear this particular silent lion's roar, we naturally need to go to a jungle, in this case to the Indian jungle nearly a thousand years ago.

We are miles from anywhere, miles from the nearest village, way out in the great aloneness of the jungle, through which there winds a path so narrow that it is very doubtful if it leads anywhere. Going along this path we see a man, quite heavily built but strong, a farmer. Nonetheless he is struggling because he is not Indian and this climate – the heat and oppressiveness of the jungle – does not suit him at all. He comes from a much colder climate. He is a Tibetan who has come down across the great barrier of the Himalayas until at last he has arrived in this sweltering place.

He is suffering, though he has been to India twice before, so he is acclimatized to some degree. He is an old hand and knows what to expect, but nevertheless he has had a hard time of it. He left his home in Tibet over two years ago, and he has endured much hardship along the road. He has spent some time in prison, locked up by a tyrannical king who took a dislike to him. But he is a very resourceful man and managed to find a way out of the situation. Now he is struggling and sweating along this jungle path. He is bent double, not with age – although he is not a young man. He is struggling and sweating and bent double because he is carrying a large leather bag. Whatever is in this bag is very heavy. He has been carrying this bag for two years now, ever since he left Tibet. He has struggled with it every step of the way. He has brought it over the highest mountains in the world. He is so used to carrying it that it has almost become a part of him.

This man whom we are watching walking along the jungle path with his heavy leather bag is called Marpa. He is a tantric teacher who has a disciple who has asked him for a teaching he does not have. This disciple is known as Great Magician. (Later he will become known as Milarepa.)[27] In order to receive the teaching for which his disciple Great Magician has asked him, Marpa is going in search of his own teacher, an Indian guru called Nāropa – the same Nāropa who many years before had abandoned Nālandā after his encounter with a ḍākinī, and has since become Enlightened through tantric meditation.

Marpa has come to India only to discover that Nāropa has vanished. He has gone into solitary retreat somewhere in the jungle. So Marpa has spent many months walking, or travelling by mule, carrying his heavy bag, trying to find his teacher. All that has kept Marpa going is that he has found another of Nāropa's disciples who has told him 'Ah, we think he is somewhere further west,' and now and again he has had a strange prophetic dream which he has interpreted as a sign of success that he will one day find Nāropa. So he struggles on. As we have said, he is a tantric guru in his own right, so he is an indomitable warrior and will not give up.

We watch Marpa as he turns a corner in the jungle path and comes upon a clearing. Seated in the middle of the clearing is Nāropa. At this stage of his life you could no longer recognize the conventional scholar-monk whom we saw at Nālandā. His encounter with Vajra-yoginī, his search for Tilopa, and his many years of study under his tantric teacher, have wrought a great change in his character and appearance. He has become gloriously free, unpredictably spontaneous, and fiercely unconventional. He is seated in the middle of this dangerous jungle practising meditation, completely unconcerned, with virtually nothing: a meditation sash, a loin cloth, and a small amount of food.

Marpa is overjoyed. He cannot believe that after two years of struggle he has finally found his teacher in the middle of this great nowhere of a jungle. He is so overcome at seeing Nāropa that he just babbles; he cannot form words. He goes up to Nāropa, throws his arms around him and embraces him. Then the combination of relief and exhaustion from his exertions overwhelms him. He falls to the ground in a faint and lies there for some time. Nāropa kindly and gently looks after him until he recovers.

When Marpa can move again he picks up the heavy leather bag he has carried so far and presents it to Nāropa. It is a leather sack with a drawstring at the top. Nāropa takes it; it is very heavy in his hand. He opens it by pulling out the drawstring and looks inside. The bag is full of gold dust.

There is a fortune in that bag that Marpa has been carrying for the last two years. There is enough gold dust for Marpa to have extended his farm, or fed all his disciples for as long as he wanted, to have bought new teachings from India, or to have supported hundreds of poor people. But he has done none of those things, he has brought it across the Himalayas, taken two years of his life, and given it to Nāropa. There is so much Nāropa can now do with it. He can support his disciples. He can build a monastery (not on the scale of Nālandā, but still quite large). He can spread the Dharma in so many ways with this gold dust that he is holding.

Nāropa is really moved. He looks into his disciple's faithful, weather-beaten face and wants to help him. Marpa's generosity inspires Nāropa to give him a very great teaching. He knows how to do it, he does not even have to think, it comes spontaneously. He holds up the big bag of gold dust, looks at it for a moment, and then with a sudden jerk throws all the gold dust into the air, turning the bag inside out. In a second there is a great cloud, an ungraspable golden cloud, filling the air all around them both.

Marpa cannot believe it; he simply cannot! It is as if his mind stops. He feels as if *he* has been turned inside out like the bag. At that point, when he feels his mind has stopped and his world has been emptied out into the sky, he has a tremendous breakthrough. Suddenly he sees something that he has never seen before....[28]

### Golden Lessons

If we may leave Nāropa and Marpa in the jungle for a little while, it is time to examine some of the implications of what we have witnessed for our own quest for freedom. When I first read this story I saw the whole incident in my mind's eye, trying to imagine what it would be like to be inside the mind and body of Marpa as he watched that shining golden cloud hanging against the blue Indian sky, reflecting the sun and yet seeming to add to it. Putting myself into the story in this way a number of ideas struck me very powerfully. I thought about value: how we give value to some things and not others; how we see gold as immensely valuable and some other things as worthless, and how this relates to their use-value for us. I reflected on how, in ultimate reality, one thing is not really more valuable than anything else; how ultimately gold is not more valuable than custard powder; how ultimately we are no more valuable than one of the mauve rhododendron flowers on the bush in the garden outside my window. But to go into all that would require a whole chapter in itself.

I reflected on how Marpa worked and sweated to accumulate the contents of that bag; how that gold was the crystallized embodiment of several years of his life, his sweat, his energy. I considered how, by extension, all material objects are embodiments of past volitions, of past efforts and straining, ideas and imagining, of the desires of different people. I became absorbed by the idea that, if you stretch your imagination, you can see the whole physical universe as the consequence of our previous actions and volitions, and about how this is especially true of our physical body; and how – if we look at the universe in this way – it can give us feedback: we can see the results of our past actions, how they have turned out, and what we can learn from that.

I found myself thinking about the qualities of gold; how it can be fashioned into any form; how you can make it into a bracelet or an adornment or a life-size statue of a man or woman, but then it can be melted down and a new form created; how it is infinitely beautiful and malleable, how it is never sullied or decayed. These qualities of gold hold reminders for me of the Buddhist view that all forms are emptiness. Not that they are all made of some stuff or substance, like gold, which then takes different forms, but that all our experience is marked with an open-ended quality that allows for infinite transformation. But to explore any of these reflections would take a chapter in itself. Instead I want to concentrate on one point, summed up in this quirky title, not 'what have you got to lose?' but '*who* have you got to lose?'

### The Nature of Fixation

By the time of this extraordinary encounter with Nāropa, Marpa has practised tantric meditation for many years, and we have seen that much tantric meditation uses symbols. Symbols are multidimensional, they show you the connectedness of things. So Marpa, looking at his bag of gold disappearing into the air, is bound to be affected on a number of different levels; he is certain to make many connections in that extraordinary moment. Marpa has spent much of his life purifying himself through the alchemy of meditation. He has turned his mind and emotions into the gold of radiant positive mental states, so that gold symbolizes his own self. But shining and positive as his mental states are, they are still limited, still attached, still tied down. Marpa's radiant consciousness is still tethered to one small location in time and space. When Nāropa empties the gold dust into the air, freeing it from the confines of the leather bag, Marpa feels as if his consciousness has been freed from the confines of the bag of his physical body. He feels free from all limitations whatsoever. He feels limitless.

Marpa has been carrying his bag for two years. All his care, all his concern has been to bring it to Nāropa. He has become very narrowly concentrated on that bag. This is the basic tendency, we can say, of saṁsāra, of conditioned existence: to be narrowed down, to be fixated, to be hypnotized by one particular object or a few particular concerns. Let us take craving as an example. What happens with craving is that your free-flowing emotional energy gets caught up with one particular person or object, and all of a sudden that is all you want – you cannot see or feel beyond it. If you try to pull your emotions away from it they come back. They have been captured, hooked. In a way, you have been hypnotized by that person or object. Equally with hatred: you become obsessed with one person or one situation. You want to eliminate, eradicate, destroy that person, that situation. This is the tendency of negative emotion, to become fixated, to become narrowed down, to become hypnotized. This happens to all of us to the extent that we are unenlightened. We all become fixated in this way, and in doing so we forget our true, limitless, sovereign, free nature.

Once upon a time there was a radiant angelic being made of golden light (such beings are called *devas* in Buddhist tradition, and they are sometimes encountered in exalted states of meditation). This deva dwelt on some mental plane that we cannot really imagine. We could think of him living in the midst of the sky perhaps – a subtle, delicate, expansive figure. He spent his time quite happily, self-possessed, perhaps occasionally mingling essences with other radiant devas.

Then, one timeless day, a strange figure appeared in the deva's world. The figure looked a little like a deva, yet his radiance had a strange quality. He seemed almost to borrow radiance from all the other devas in order to appear very bright. He looked a somewhat out-of-place traveller in those realms of beauty. He was a kind of pedlar, and he too carried a bag. In this bag he had all sorts of very bright, colourful, but worthless things. He tried to attract the attention of the golden deva.

The deva was not really attracted to this being at all, but he wanted to be welcoming, for his nature was expansive and innocent. So he gave a small proportion of his vast span of attention – which flooded out across space – to the pedlar, who began producing things from his bag – bright colourful things – and waving them in front of him. Occasionally, from out of his beautiful reverie, the deva would notice a few of these colourful fripperies, but he took no more than a polite and passing interest in them.

The pedlar kept up his efforts to interest the deva. After several failures he produced from the depths of his bag one last item. It was a wooden puppet, dressed in a sort of tattered cloak, and sewn on its surface were hundreds of little sequins and broken pieces of mirror. He held this up in front of the deva and began to swing it like a pendulum. At first, the deva again was not all that interested but out of politeness and out of the feeling of freedom which devas have – that everything in the universe is your friend because you pervade most of the universe – he became engaged in looking at the little puppet dangling from its strings in the hands of the pedlar.

As the little puppet swung from side to side, side to side, the mirrors on its cloak reflected the beautiful golden light of the deva, which caused him to pay proper attention for the first time to the pedlar's antics. The deva was not self-conscious in any egotistical sense – he had no sense of 'I am beautiful', he was quite innocent – so seeing this beautiful golden light and thinking it came from the puppet he become more and more involved. The pedlar continued swinging the puppet from side to side, the light seemed to shine from it, and the pedlar began talking in a very soft, steady, rhythmic tone of voice.

He told the deva how beautiful the puppet was and how good it would be if one could be like this puppet shining with golden light. He talked on and on, urging the deva to come nearer and nearer.... 'Look at the puppet. Do not pay attention to anything else. Just look at the puppet. You can be the puppet. You can go into the puppet. You're going into the puppet. You *are* this puppet. And now I can work you with the strings in my hand. I can put you into my bag. I can carry you away and your golden light has vanished.'

We are all like the radiant deva. We have all been hypnotized into taking the tattered puppet's form of a human being. Even though now we feel dissatisfied, we feel trapped and imprisoned. Strangely, we have become afraid of freedom. We are scared of our own limitless potential. We suffer from a kind of spiritual agoraphobia and will not go into the wide open spaces of consciousness which are our true home.

According to Buddhist tradition, as described, for example, in *The Tibetan Book of the Dead*,[29] we repeat this pattern over lifetimes. When one puppet body falls apart and for a little while we experience that freedom once more – when the clear light of Reality dawns – we become terrified and run away. We ask the strange pedlar to provide us, please, with another puppet in which we can feel safe, which will occupy all our attention. However, this analogy is limited. There is no outside entity, no pedlar who creates for us a new physical body, with its limited senses and liability to old age, sickness, and death. The tragedy is that this is something we do to ourselves, a way in which we organize our consciousness.

### Breaking the Spell

How can we break the spell? How can we stop being hypnotized by what is limited and unsatisfying? How can we overcome the fear of the vastness of our own true nature? We have to start by seeing that this is the situation, that we have been cheated, or rather that we have cheated ourselves of the unlimited freedom that is our true birthright. Whatever it may take, we have to commit ourselves to working to regain that freedom, that limitlessness which we really are.

The commitment to regain that freedom is Going for Refuge. That commitment must express itself in practice. In particular I want to look at two practices that will free us from the limitations we have imposed on ourselves. One is meditation; the other is generosity.

In order to see how meditation and generosity can help us, we need first a clear picture of what has taken place. In simple terms, what has happened is that we have confined ourselves within a boundary. This boundary we usually call 'I'. Everything outside the boundary is 'other' or alien. We tend for some strange reason to think of this boundary as fixed, although if we examine it we soon find it is not. Usually the sense of boundary, the sense of 'I', is associated with control; everything we can control is 'I'; everything we cannot control is 'out there'. However, if we look at the boundaries of what we can control, it soon becomes clear that they are constantly shifting.

Sometimes we can control other people and objects, and sometimes we cannot control aspects of ourselves.

If you wake up in the morning and you have been lying on your arm, you find that it is completely dead, and when you try to move it nothing happens. You have to pull it out from under the pillow and shake it, you have no control over it. Sometimes in meditation you tell yourself to count ten breaths. Useless! Your mind has other ideas, which it pursues like a dog ignoring its owner's calls. You do not control that either.

Our ego-boundary, which we want to be fixed and secure, is shifting all the time. We can feel very insecure when we are made aware that this is the case. We often prefer to identify our boundaries with those of the physical body, because although that does change, it usually does so quite slowly. Though we know that our cells change every seven years, the body at least gives an illusion of a permanent being within whose secure boundary we can anchor our feelings and thoughts. So, in a way, our skin becomes our boundary, the limit of 'I', the frontier of 'me'. It is our sense of touch that gives us our feeling of solidity, our basic point of self-reference.

Touch and taste are the most limited and localized of our senses. Maybe that is why, when we are not feeling very happy, not feeling expansive, we turn particularly to those two senses. We turn to taste for gratification through food or drink. And we turn to touch for a warm cuddle, for sex, or for that secure feeling when we bury ourselves under the duvet. When we feel lighter and more expansive we move into the other senses. They give us information from further away. With smell we can perhaps take in things that happen across the garden. With hearing we can sometimes hear events miles away. Hearing can carry us out of ourselves, like Keats listening to the nightingale, or Shelley to the skylark. With sight we can see part of the way across the universe, we can view events that have happened light years away.

This suggests a hierarchy of the senses. Some are more expansive than others. It is perhaps for this reason that Buddhist visualization practice concentrates almost entirely on hearing and on sight – these are the two main senses that are involved through mantra and visualization of different Buddha and Bodhisattva forms. These two senses are the most expansive. They lead us furthest away from a preoccupation with one localized point in space. This is one reason why meditation is so effective. Through meditation we can explore and expand our boundaries.

If you become concentrated on your breath in meditation you may find yourself naturally exploring the nature of your ego-boundary. Your attention may become poised on the very tip of your nose, at the first point where the air from 'outside' touches the skin that is 'you'. You are right on that frontier. Where do you begin and end? As you become increasingly absorbed in the experience, it becomes harder and harder to say.

If you practise meditation on loving-kindness, you expand the emotion from yourself outward and outward, including more and more people and other forms of life. Eventually you may almost forget yourself completely. You become a cloud of friendliness, of love and well-wishing, expanding outwards into space. Meditation brings us up against what we think are our boundaries, and enables our consciousness to expand beyond them.

Something else happens in meditation that affects this way in which we fixate or hypnotize ourselves. In deep meditation discursive thought stops. Why is it that we think more or less from the moment we wake up until last thing at night? All through the day there are usually trains of discursive thought rumbling through our minds. Why does this happen? It happens because, in a way, we are afraid. We are like children talking to ourselves or whistling in the dark to keep our spirits up, because reality is constantly threatening to break in on us. We are constantly in danger of waking up from the hypnotic trance, of discovering again that we are really radiant devas after all. But we are scared of that; we have forgotten what it is like. We are used to being puppets in tattered cloaks. So we keep talking to ourselves all day and every day, over and over like the soft voice of the hypnotist, and we start most of our sentences with 'I'. 'I need …', 'I want …'. We hypnotize ourselves. We fixate ourselves on this supposedly fixed thing called 'I'.

But you can only be hypnotized in this way if you decide to be. Someone who has found true freedom is not suggestible, cannot be hypnotized, does not get fixated. Our limited world only continues, the hypnotic trance only carries on, because we want it to. If we allow the train of discursive thought to cease for a while, or if we start to see its empty nature, extraordinary changes can follow.

Through meditation we can refine and expand our consciousness. We can also arrive at a state of deep concentration where the mental discourse that reinforces our limited conditioning stops. When that happens, when there is a gap in what we are constantly telling ourselves about the world, there arises the possibility, at least for a while, of reality breaking in, and our awakening to our true expansiveness. Meditation is very valuable indeed. It is the alchemy that can turn the dross of our minds into pure gold.

In order to complete the process of freeing ourselves we need also to give. We need to open our hearts and offer what we have to others. This can be simply material aid and assistance; on a deeper level, we can give of ourselves – to our work, to our friends, to life – as the Bodhisattva is a resource for living beings. Every time we give we move beyond ourselves. Each act of giving helps us break through the limitations created by our sense of separate selfhood. Generosity is an affirmation that the boundary between ourselves and the world is ultimately illusory. Marpa does not just give Nāropa a fortune in gold dust, he offers himself – body, speech, and mind – to his teacher. In giving himself completely he is freed completely.

### Unlimited Consciousness

Meditation and generosity are two aspects of one process. Our lives can become a constant process of going within in meditation, mining the gold within us and giving that gold out to other people, to life. According to Buddhist legend, the texts of the Perfection of Wisdom, which describe the way of thinking of someone who has gained transcendental experience, were preserved for many centuries by the *nāgas*. Nāgas are water spirits who have some of the qualities of dragons. Like dragons, they are also guardians of treasure. In some Buddhist texts the nāgas are guardians of wisdom; they hold the texts which describe how to achieve understanding of Reality. It is as if, in order to find wisdom, we have to dive far down within ourselves, deep into the ocean of the mind, to the palace where the nāgas dwell. We have to take the gold from them and share it with all living beings. If we continue this process of diving deep inside and then venturing outwards, we shall eventually find that inside and outside have become indivisible. Then we shall see that what we identified with, what we thought of as 'me', was the conflict at the boundary between our inner and outer worlds. The ego is the product of the tension, the friction, between the vast outer universe and the boundless depths of the universe within. Its demands, which usually drown out everything else, are just the noise of the ocean waves of our 'inner world' breaking against the shore of the 'external world'.

The busy thoughts and feelings with which we identify tend to be responses to conflict. In a situation in which what happens to you conflicts strongly with what you want, or with deep currents of feeling in your inner world, you are usually very stirred up. Your mind begins to whirl. You try to find ways to bring what you want into existence in the outer world. Strong feelings are produced in you. You become painfully aware of 'you'. But when your inner world and your outer world harmonize, your mind becomes quiet, your feelings become gentle, and your sense of yourself becomes subtle and refined. Through practising meditation and generosity it is possible to do away with the conflict between inner and outer altogether, to resolve the tension between the two. You are no longer fixated. Your consciousness ceases to be limited. You have broken the spell. You have recovered your true, limitless, free nature.

Nāropa's sudden emptying of that gold into the air, his silent but resounding lion's roar, has pointed out a great deal to us. It has shown us that we are all free and unlimited but that we have become fixated, hypnotized, limited to one point in space and time. By Going for Refuge we commit ourselves to breaking the trance, overcoming our habitual fear of expansion and moving beyond the illusory barriers between self and other. To do this we have two chief tools at our disposal. Firstly, meditation, which refines and expands us and enables us to cut off the mental dialogue with which we reinforce our fixation. Secondly, generosity, through which we open our hearts and break down the sense of separate fixed selfhood which imprisons us.

If we persevere on the path to freedom, if we practise meditation and generosity with increasing energy, then one day we shall stand where Marpa stood. We shall know how he felt as he stood amazed, gazing at that ungraspable cloud of gold dust shining in the air above him. We shall understand the feelings of two tantric warriors alone in a dangerous jungle, of whom one has given away a fortune and the other has literally thrown it away. We shall know how they feel as they sit and watch the gold fall from the sky and start to settle on their hands, clothes, and hair, covering them in gold, beginning to cover the leaves of the forest clearing. We shall understand as they become two golden figures, two golden people in a golden clearing. We shall understand as having lost a fortune they look at each other and laugh like children. For they know that they are not two poor separate individuals. The spell is broken. The barriers are down. They are infinitely wealthy, rich in radiant golden consciousness.

# PART FOUR

Zen Buddhism

# 8

# Facing the Tiger

## Zen and the Tiger's Cave

In our final three chapters we shall be watching dramatic demonstrations of how to live freely from the Zen Buddhist tradition. Like Tibetan Buddhism, Zen follows the Mahāyāna tradition, emphasizing the Bodhisattva ideal of working to gain Enlightenment for the sake of all living beings. The word *Zen* is Japanese and relates to the Chinese word *ch'an* which, in its turn, comes from the Sanskrit word *dhyāna*, meaning meditation. From this you can gather that Zen is a form of Buddhism that came to Japan via China and which focuses particularly on meditative experience. There is a famous short verse that sums up what Zen is about, and its first two lines are

> *A direct transmission outside the scriptures;*
> *No dependence on words and letters.*[30]

From these lines you will see that Zen is not much concerned with the rational mind. Through meditation it aims to take you to a level of experience that is not dependent on rational explanations. Zen is characterized by very strong, direct teaching methods which are designed to give no foothold for your intellect. It works to undermine any sense that you can sum up life and reality in concepts. Zen rubs your nose in direct experience.

Zen training is very disciplined. As we have seen, it places a strong emphasis on meditation, usually including a great deal of sitting meditation, which is known as *zazen*. It uses this disciplined training to arrive at a state of spontaneity and freedom. This will become clearer from these stories.

The three incidents we shall be exploring in these chapters were all collected by Trevor Leggett, an Englishman who is a seventh dan in judo and has also studied and practised Zen meditation. He has written several books on Buddhism, and I have always very much appreciated his work. These stories are taken from a book which in later editions is called *A Second Zen Reader*, but whose original title was *The Tiger's Cave*.[31] Imagine that in a remote part of the jungle there is a cave. If there happens to be a tiger in this cave, there might be many animal tracks, perhaps even human footprints, going into it, but none coming out.... Thus the tiger's cave suggests an experience that many people enter and from which no one returns. In Zen, this becomes a symbol for insight into Reality, for understanding the true nature of yourself and your life. This insight into Reality, we have seen, is the crucial point on the Buddhist path, the beginning of unending freedom.

If you were to venture into a tiger's cave, the chances are that you would die there. Insight into Reality is also a kind of spiritual death. As we have seen, if you follow the path to freedom sincerely, at a certain point you come to an experience in which you realize that what you thought you were is a fabrication, that the fixed 'I' standing behind your experience, which you are constantly protecting, does not ultimately exist. The tiger's cave is a symbol for this experience, in which the sense of fixed, separate selfhood disappears. It is not that you have a fixed, unchanging 'I' which is then dissolved away. Rather, in the insight experience you realize that this separate selfhood was a fiction, a deeply-held wrong notion. So nothing really dies in the tiger's cave. However, we all hold so tightly and fiercely to this sense of inherent existence, and we feel so much anxiety and insecurity when it is threatened, that this 'death of a wrong notion' has a profoundly liberating effect.

### Three Men and a Korean Export

This story takes place in Japan, some time in the seventeenth century. We do not know exactly when, but an educated guess would suggest around 1643. Before we look at the incident itself, it will be helpful to have some idea of the background, and of the main characters involved. Until about 1600 there had been a great deal of strife in

Japan, but this is now a fairly quiet period in Japanese life, during which people are able to concentrate more on the arts and meditation. However, society is still dominated by the hereditary military dictators of the Tokugawa Shōgunate. The present Shōgun, Iemitsu, is the most influential person in the entire country, far more so than the Emperor, but he is quite young to be holding the power of life and death over so many people. At the time of our story he cannot be older than 21, and is perhaps still in his teens.[32] Understandably, as a military dictator surrounded by samurai warriors, who live and often die by the sword, Iemitsu has a very strong interest in preserving and developing the tradition of swordsmanship – *kendō*. To this end he has several fencing masters.

The Shōgun's chief fencing master is an old samurai called Yagyū. (He does not know it yet, but he will die in 1646.) For Yagyū to have become the fencing master of the Shōgun he must be both a very accomplished swordsman and a strong character. Yagyū is also a student of Zen Buddhism, and is practising zazen. The teaching of Zen at this time needs to be quite simple, because most people cannot understand its classical texts. Instead, they have to be taught the Dharma in very direct ways, by being presented with situations from their own experience. Being a samurai and a fencing master naturally provides Yagyū with much material for meditation on issues of life and death.

As well as fencing, the Shōgun is himself very interested in Buddhism, and has a number of Dharma teachers. Among these is Takuan Sōhō, one of the greatest Zen Buddhist masters of his time. He was born in 1573, so he too is getting on in years – he must be about 70. Although he is old, there is still a sense of powerful but controlled energy about him. A great popularizer of Zen, he has tried to create forms of Buddhism that people will find directly relevant to their lives. He is a popular figure around the court, and is having a great effect on the arts and cultural life. As well as being in favour with Iemitsu, he is also the Buddhist teacher of several of the Shōgun's fencing masters, including Yagyū. In fact, Takuan wrote a long letter of advice to Yagyū which has been preserved and which we shall come to later. It is one of the most interesting Japanese documents we possess from this period.

Takuan (whose name, incidentally, is Japanese for 'pickled radish') does not know this yet either, but he is going to die in 1645, a year before Yagyū. On his deathbed he will be requested by the people around him to write something – a last piece of advice. It is very common in the Zen tradition to ask a master to write a few lines that sum up his experience as he is facing death. Some of these death poems are very interesting indeed. When Takuan was asked for one of these he resisted. However, the people persisted in their request, so he finally took brush and ink, wrote just one ideogram, and passed away. His death poem was the word 'dream'.

There is one more character who will play a major part in this story – if you can call him, her, or it, a character. In the grounds of the Shōgun's residence lives a very large tiger. This great animal has been captured in Korea and brought to Japan in a cage. As far as I am aware, tigers were not native to Japan, so the tiger has presumably been brought from abroad specially for the Shōgun to see. Importing exotic animals was a common practice at this time. For instance, somewhat earlier, in England, Henry VII kept a number of leopards.

It is interesting to imagine what it would be like to live in a country where you had only heard about tigers as fabulous beasts, and then to see this powerful striped animal prowling up and down its cage, with its great head and fierce eyes. It would be almost like something coming from another dimension into your world, equivalent to us, perhaps, seeing a dragon. Tigers became very common artistic subjects in Japan. I remember in my early twenties seeing a hanging scroll of a tiger by Kishi Ganku which I found extraordinary. In a way it did not look like a tiger at all, in terms of anatomy. It seemed almost boneless, and yet the artist had captured a kind of essence of tiger, and made every hair on its body stand out.[33]

### The Shōgun's Challenge

Our story takes place on a beautiful summer's day. The Shōgun is sitting outside his residence, surrounded by his entourage, among whom are Yagyū and Takuan. They are sitting near the tiger's cage, after a visit to inspect the newly-arrived beast. Noises from the cage occasionally punctuate the party's conversation, which is mainly concerned with how much can be achieved by someone who is highly-trained in kendō. The way of the sword is not just about footwork, speed, and timing. It involves honing your being, your will, so that when you meet an opponent you may even subdue him with a look or a shout, leaving him beaten before you move your sword.

This conversation (and another roar from the cage) give the Shō-gun an idea. He wonders aloud, just out of interest, whether it would be possible for someone like Yagyū who has trained for many years in the way of the sword to enter the tiger's cage – without his sword, but taking that fan he has with him – and then to use his skills as a swordsman to touch the tiger's head. The Shōgun's word is law. His 'wondering' is an absolute command, particularly in a society that sets great store by not 'losing face'.

Yagyū bows to the Shōgun, and the whole party moves down towards the tiger. They all distribute themselves near the iron cage where they can see what happens, with the Shōgun seated in the middle. Yagyū looks at the tiger through the bars. It is very large....

However, the Shōgun's word is a command, and Yagyū owes him complete allegiance. He picks up his fan and walks slowly towards the cage. As he does so the tiger's keeper, alerted to what he is about to do, comes forward. This man has travelled with the tiger, caring for it and feeding it. He knows it better than anyone. He warns Yagyū that to attempt to enter the cage and face the tiger empty-handed is madness. Yagyū ignores the man and walks purposefully to the door of the cage. He withdraws the bolt, opens the door, and goes in to face the tiger.

Yagyū has looked death in the eye before. Many men have tried to kill him, but then he always had his sword, and his skills were honed against human opponents, knowing what to expect, when to parry, when to move. This animal brought from another country is com-pletely outside his experience. All he can do is use his skills to try to dominate the tiger, which is looking at him with an unreadable expression from across the cage. He must summon up all his will-power and hold the beast under his sway, as he moves forwards very slowly and carefully, all the time looking the tiger in the eye. It growls. But he is not listening to that, he is focusing on holding the great beast as strongly as he can with his will. He moves closer, and in his mind it is a sword, not a fan, that he holds in front of him. The tiger growls again, but Yagyū does not falter. Now he is very close ... and now he can just reach out and ... touch the tiger. He feels the sensation of the soft fur under his sweating palm.

The scent of the animal, and the knowledge, forcibly suppressed, of what its claws and teeth could do to him, bring fear close to the surface of his mind. Yagyū fights it back. Still holding the tiger with his gaze he withdraws his hand and begins moving backwards – in slow measured steps – towards the door. (He knows exactly where the door is; his years of training have given him a highly-developed spatial awareness.) But the tiger is still there in front of him, and he is not safe yet. Yagyū is too experienced to make the mistake of relaxing before a contest is over. Still retreating very slowly he comes to the door, and in one flowing movement slips through, pulls it shut, and bolts it.

Yagyū turns and walks away, bathed in sweat. He goes back to the Shōgun and bows. The Shōgun is really quite taken with that demonstration of the skills of swordsmanship. He is generous in his praise. That was very good indeed. Yes, most impressive. It shows what years of training can achieve. But now he wonders ... the Zen master Takuan is, after all, a teacher of Zen, and Buddhism claims to go far beyond the way of the sword. So the Shōgun wonders whether perhaps Zen has something else to show us? And of course that is a command as well!

Takuan, in his grey robe, has been sitting quietly. He has watched Yagyū – his friend and student whom he has taught for many years – facing the tiger. Takuan is quite proud of him and the fine spirit he has shown, though there is still much room for improvement.... Now the Shōgun's 'Does Zen have anything else to show us?' has turned the spotlight on him. How can he respond?

Without a thought, Takuan leaps up from his seat and starts running towards the tiger's cage. You can see the sleeves of his robe flapping as he moves down the path. He comes to the door of the cage, pulls open the bolt, and jumps inside as if he were going to greet a long-lost friend. He strides across the cage until he is within arm's reach of the tiger. Then he spits on his hand, and holds it out in front of him. He can feel the animal's warm breath on his outstretched palm. The tiger sniffs his hand carefully, and then licks it! Delicate shivers run up Takuan's arm from the sensations of that rough tongue on his hand. He pats the great furry head in a friendly way. Then he turns around and strolls calmly out of the cage, mindfully bolting the door after him.

The Shōgun is dumbfounded. When he can find his voice, he says, 'After all, our way of the sword cannot compete with Zen.'

### The World of Scissors and Rock

It might be best just to leave you to meditate on this story. Imagine yourself as the Shōgun; as the fencing master; as Takuan; as the tiger. Put yourself into the sandals of Takuan as he runs down to the cage. How do you feel? Nonetheless, I would like to share with you a few reflections, from living out the story in my own imagination.

Our four main characters all inhabit very different worlds, although three of them live, in varying ways, in the world of power and control. None of the three is entirely secure, because in the world of power and control one can never make oneself entirely safe. One may try very hard, but it is an impossible task because of the very nature of that world. Thus each of the three has undoubted strengths, and inevitable weaknesses. The Shōgun is the most powerful person in Japan. He can call on an army of warriors, order men to their deaths, but if he were ever to enter the tiger's cage the Shōgun would not stand a chance. Yagyū the swordsman can control the tiger by sheer force of will, but if the Shōgun turns against him and orders his death or banishment, his skills will avail him nothing. The tiger is sheer physical power and strength. Let loose it can create havoc, but once captured and caged its life is forfeit.

This situation is like that game, called *jenkan* in Japanese, in which two players simultaneously hold out a hand, making the shape of scissors, rock, or paper. Each can overcome one of the others, but each in its turn is beaten by one of the others. Scissors cut paper but are blunted by rock, and so on. Everyone in that world has a certain amount of power; but they have also their weaknesses, and therefore their insecurities.

These three also seem to me to represent, very broadly, different aspects of the human psyche, different forces at play in human life:

The tiger is instinctual nature, which is very powerful and not to be underestimated. Until this instinctual energy is well tamed, for want of a better word – brought into harmony with the rest of our being – it will be very hard for us to gain emotional stability or deep happiness. Sooner or later we have to confront the instinctual energies in ourselves and engage them in our quest for freedom, otherwise we can easily swing between extremes. Most of the time we stand well back from those energies and live quite a positive life: following the precepts, but not very engaged or energized. This rather bloodless state is punctuated by occasional outbursts of mayhem where, with a growl, we shrug off all our intellectual ideas about Buddhism, following the precepts, and meditation. After one of these sudden swings it may take us some time to get the tiger back into the cage.

The Shōgun represents the egotistic tendency to hold life at a distance. He sits surrounded by his entourage, moving people around like chessmen, manipulating the situation. He is always in control. He remains at a safe distance from the tiger. We too tend to have a part of ourselves that subtly uses power to manipulate others to do our bidding. Operating in this way we often manage to create what feels like a secure world for ourselves, in which we stand at a distance and keep everything under control. This is true of our relations with others. It is also true of our relations with our own deeper, more instinctual energies on the early stages of the path to freedom. Somehow we manage to ignore the roars of the tiger, which symbolize the parts of ourselves that we cannot control. Nonetheless, those roars and growls still register somewhere, and we know deep down that when we act in this way we are not finally secure. We can never feel safe if we have had to cage up part of ourselves.

What does Yagyū the fencing master represent? He is very self-disciplined, and is practising meditation under Takuan's guidance. Thus he stands for someone who is following the path to freedom, in the process of freeing himself but not yet fully free. He represents a tremendous step forward from the ego-control of the Shōgun. Yagyū is able to confront the wildness of the tiger, so he symbolizes a stage of the path where we have begun to bridge the rational and the instinctual. To find our freedom we have to understand what the Dharma is as clearly as possible, and then take that understanding into an encounter with our own strongest energies. Our intellect, which at first is often used in the service of control and for holding life at a distance, now becomes engaged in an active exploration of our experience.

In striving for freedom, Yagyū is spurred on by his warrior's awareness of death, which gives his life great strength. If we manage to live with the possibility of death – our own and that of people around us – it undermines our sense that we can keep everything under control – the ego's feeling that it holds sway, that it has everything arranged. Living with death reminds us of the ever-present prospect of transformation.

Although he is making impressive efforts on the path to freedom, Yagyū has yet to arrive at insight into reality. He is still within the world of egotistic concerns, and hence still in the world of power and control, and of insecurity. He temporarily subdues the tiger; he does not befriend it. He represents, if you like, the ego working at its limits, striving for a freedom which it still believes it can attain.

Whilst these three are all in the world of power and control in different ways, Takuan has gone beyond it altogether. Through many years of valiant meditation and devoted Buddhist practice, he has seen through egotistic concern for security and left that world behind.[34] He lives in the world of wisdom, which is also the world of transcendental love and complete freedom. Thus he can run to meet the tiger without a first thought, let alone any second ones.

In Takuan the battle between reason and instinctual energy is over. This means he can move happily between worlds. He can spend time in the retinue of the Shōgun, conversing with the most powerful man in Japan, and then leap up and run down to the tiger's cage. He is happy sitting with his companions, he is happy to meet the tiger, he is a friend to all living beings. He does not really feel separate from anything in the universe. Everything he does is an expression of the Dharma, and he is infinitely adaptable. He communicates to both the Shōgun and the tiger in their own language. To the Shōgun and his companions he speaks the language of words, of art, and of culture. With the great cat he spits on his hand. That is the Dharma teaching for the tiger!

### How to Swallow Frogs

The tiger in our story can take on other symbolic meanings. It can stand quite simply for whatever we avoid. It is helpful on the path to freedom to ask ourselves regularly, 'What am I avoiding? What do I tend to steer clear of in my practice of the Dharma?' It is good to ask this with regard to ordinary life situations, looking at jobs we put off, and people we skirt around. It is also important to explore this question in relation to specific Dharma practices. For example, we may find that in meditation we really enjoy concentrating on our breath, but somehow we never get around to the cultivation of loving-kindness. There may be certain precepts whose implications for our lives we never seriously consider. When we find ourselves side-stepping in this way, we have to do our best, however falteringly, to take steps to face the tiger. I find it helpful to reflect on the maxim 'If you do not deal with life, it will deal with you.' We all have aspects of our lives with which we would rather not engage. Very often it is only when we start facing them squarely that we realize how much of a negative and undermining effect our avoidance has been having. We may put a lot of effort into some areas, but if there is a hole in our practice then inevitably energy will drain away. We shall never be truly free if there are aspects of life from which we are on the run.

Facing tigers is not easy, and very often it is only when we see that we have no alternative, through experiencing the painful consequences of our avoidance, that we start moving towards the tiger's cage. Facing our own tiger, whatever it may be, is very often the fastest way to transform ourselves as human beings. It is easy to keep circling some crucial aspect of our life or character without addressing it. We may sometimes need to be strategic about setting up the right conditions for facing our tiger, though we must not use this as an excuse for procrastination but make sure that we are moving steadily towards it. Perhaps Takuan's running to meet the tiger can provide us with a lesson. We may be better off not giving ourselves too much time to think before facing situations we would rather avoid. As Mark Twain wrote, 'If you have to swallow two frogs, swallow the big one first, and don't look at it too long.'

Takuan can move freely because he has dealt with life and death. He has gained insight into their true nature and seen that they are both like a dream, as in the poem that he wrote on his deathbed. Takuan knows that the Shōgun, Yagyū, the tiger, and himself do not finally, inherently exist. The tiger is a dream tiger (although those teeth will look real enough to anyone in the cage). Through this wisdom he has become detached from the cares and worries of life, but that does not stop him being actively engaged in it. Through compassion, through transcendental friendliness, he cares for everything around him. Because his insight has melted the iceberg of an imagined self which has to be protected, which stands apart from everything else, Takuan flows through life freely, and deals with it directly.

*Spontaneity – the Quality You Cannot Decide to Produce*
Before we conclude this chapter we shall look at two related aspects of freedom that Takuan exhibits: alacrity and spontaneity. To give you a sense of these and the part they play in Zen, here is an extract from the letter that Takuan wrote to Yagyū about fencing. He says

> What is most important in the art of fencing is to acquire a certain mental attitude known as 'immovable wisdom'. This wisdom is intuitively acquired after a great deal of practical training. 'Immovable' does not mean to be stiff and heavy and lifeless as a rock or a piece of wood. It means the highest degree of motility with a centre which remains immovable. The mind then reaches the highest point of alacrity ready to direct its attention anywhere it is needed – to the left, to the right, to all the directions as required. When your attention is engaged and arrested by the striking sword of the enemy, you lose the first opportunity of making the next move by yourself. You tarry, you think, and while this deliberation goes on, your opponent is ready to strike you down. The thing is not to give him such a chance. You must follow the movement of the sword in the hands of the enemy, leaving your mind free to make its own counter-movement.... There is something immovable within, which, however, moves along spontaneously with things presenting themselves before it. The mirror of wisdom reflects them instantaneously one after another, keeping itself intact and undisturbed. The fencer must cultivate this.[35]

In this letter Takuan is talking about fencing, but what he says holds true for life in general. Though aware of and engaged in the fight, the fencer must also cultivate detachment, his awareness must not 'stick' at any point. Rather it must reflect everything that is happening – like a cinema screen. The screen does not favour some characters more than others. It does not prevent the film moving freely. If we develop this 'immovable wisdom', then our undisturbed mind will move freely, dancing perfectly in time with the objects that come before it, reflecting whatever is there, and not sticking anywhere. It is craving and aversion that cause our minds to stick and thus to falter in the dance. Takuan illustrates the spontaneity of this immovable wisdom, saying it is like clapping your hands together. The sound does not think about coming out, it is just there.

Spontaneity is not a quality you can try to produce directly. It will not work to think 'I must be spontaneous,' because, as Takuan points out, this self-conscious 'spontaneity' is just another way of sticking, another idea that removes you from the flow of life.

Paradoxically, true spontaneity arises out of dedicated, disciplined effort. We arrive at spontaneous skilful action through careful practice of the five precepts, which we examined in Chapter 1. We contact the flowing and free quality of life, through putting ourselves deeply in touch with our experience through awareness practices such as meditation on the breath. We arrive at spontaneous love, compassion, and equanimity, through steady and continuing work with our feelings, replacing negative emotions with loving-kindness. Finally we arrive at spontaneous understanding of the nature of reality, through repeated reflection on subjects like impermanence and absence of inherent existence.

In all these practices, consistency is vital. This is why Zen uses disciplined training to arrive at spontaneity. If we make only occasional efforts at Buddhist practices we shall hardly obtain any results. At best we may learn what they have to teach us on a rational level. To absorb their lessons into our being requires regularity and repetition, like a fencer practising the same parry and riposte again and again. It is only when their movements become natural and unthinking that a fencer achieves mastery. Similarly, it is only when the lessons of our repeated Buddhist practices have become second nature that we shall arrive at spontaneous freedom.

Without disciplined practice over quite a number of years, 'being spontaneous' usually means giving way to the whims at the surface of your mind. It is easy to follow your everyday likes and dislikes and imagine you are exhibiting spontaneity in the positive sense. But for Buddhism spontaneity is something which emerges from a mind cleared of craving and aversion. When Takuan goes to meet the tiger he has no plan in his head about what he will do. He goes into the cage and out of the depths of himself there arises an instant response to the situation, to the great animal in front of him. He spits on his hand and holds it out to the tiger. Takuan is completely spontaneous, and you cannot fake spontaneity. If someone were to copy him by running down to the tiger's cage, and leaping in, what would happen? Their being 'spontaneous' would be another predetermined idea. The tiger would sense it, and rather than licking their hand would be licking its lips, happy that lunch had arrived!

Although spontaneity is a product of spiritual training, and cannot be forced, there is something we can do to encourage its appearance. We can work at holding our ideas about ourselves much more lightly, and constantly looking at life afresh. This applies particularly to keeping an open mind about where meditation and Buddhism should be taking us. As we meditate, we shall change in ways that we could never have imagined. If we could predict exactly how we were going to be in five years' time we would be spiritually dead. We would just be changing, not transforming ourselves. Through making a disciplined effort to practise the precepts and to meditate regularly, we shall find that the unexpected arises spontaneously. It can be inspiring to realize that Enlightenment will be different from anything we can imagine for ourselves now, altogether better and finer than anything we could have predicted.

*Ignoring Freud and Acting with Alacrity*
We cannot try to be spontaneous, but we can consciously develop the related quality of alacrity, which is a lively responsiveness – being prepared to respond to what needs doing without holding back. Alacrity means leaping in to a situation, just as old Takuan raced to the tiger's cage with the sleeves of his robe flapping as he ran. In Zen this is called *mo chi chu*, which roughly translated means 'going right ahead without stopping'. To develop this quality we have to train ourselves not to listen to the enervating voices of self-doubt. All too often, people have some positive impulse and then talk themselves out of it. They were going to give, they were going to help ... but then the voice of self-doubt whispered to them, and they decided it was better to play safe and not become involved.

The voices of self-doubt have become louder since the discoveries of Freud. Learning that we have motivations of which we are not conscious (and that very often those motivations are not very positive) can all too easily make us suspicious of ourselves. We have an impulse to give, to help, but then we begin to think, 'Yes, but why do I want to do this? Perhaps I am being egotistical. If I volunteer to do this maybe people will think I want to be noticed or I consider myself to be special. Perhaps that is my motivation. Maybe I shouldn't do it.' There are many ways like this in which we may hack at the little sprouts of our positive volitions, undercutting them by questioning our motivation, thinking, 'Well, I am probably not doing this for the right reasons.'

We would be better off taking our positive actions at face value. Obviously we do need to be aware of our motivation, and I am not advocating naïvety. But if we feel the urge to do something positive, rather than undermining ourselves by ferreting about for unconscious motivations, we would usually be better off straightforwardly going ahead. Then we shall cultivate alacrity in doing what is positive. If we put too many mental obstacles and cross-examinations of ourselves in the way of our positive responses we shall block our energy. Ideally, seeing the good should flow naturally into action.

The Freudian legacy can also make us mistrustful of people who appear to be doing something positive. Someone gives a large amount of money to a hospital and people think, 'Oh they wanted to have their name put on a plaque, so they would be remembered.' (If it was an anonymous donation, then people assume the donor must feel really guilty about something, to need to salve their conscience by giving like that!) Rather than wondering about what is in it for them, we would do better simply to applaud them. If their action is appreciated, any mixed motive they may have will in time probably be rectified, because people generally respond to appreciation by becoming more positive. Overall, life will go better if we give ourselves and others the benefit of the doubt.

If we practise acting with alacrity we shall not hesitate when life confronts us with difficult challenges. We shall have the momentum to go straight ahead without stopping, as Takuan ran to meet the tiger. As we keep jumping into different situations we shall learn to face what we used to hang back from and avoid. We shall develop the capacity to meet life more than half way.

I have been interpreting this story as if it was a myth, or a legend, with different characters representing different aspects of the psyche. However, we should not forget that Yagyū and Takuan were human beings like us. We too have the potential to develop to the point where even a very large tiger, even the prospect of death, does not bother us. We may never meet a tiger, but all of us, one day, will have to face death in one form or another – so it is vital to bear in mind that if we make the effort to work creatively with our minds, as Takuan did year after year, we will reach a point where we understand the true nature of life. Then we shall face death freely, happily, with our robes flapping in the wind as we run down to the cage. Takuan's alacrity, his spirit of meeting life more than half way, is something we need to remember if we are to progress on the path to freedom, because, as we have seen, if you don't deal with life, life will deal with you.

# 9

# A Small Glass of Wine

*Hiding a Fugitive*

The last chapter saw us in seventeenth-century Japan, where both Yagyū and Takuan faced the tiger with the spontaneity and alacrity that are important aspects of true freedom. This time we remain in Japan, but we have moved forward to the nineteenth century, as we look at another story from Trevor Leggett's *The Tiger's Cave*.[36] This story, too, involves a life-threatening event. Many Zen stories deal with commonplace incidents, but because Zen focuses very directly on our existential situation and how we resolve the basic human issue – life and death – it is particularly interested in situations where someone who has gained insight into Reality through their Buddhist training faces death or danger.

During this time in Japan there are many civil disturbances. In one of the areas where there is much fighting and unrest is a Zen temple, whose abbot is called Bokusan. One day, there is a skirmish between rival groups in the area, and one of the samurai on the losing side flees for his life. He knows his pursuers are not far behind him, and he desperately needs a refuge, a sanctuary from their swords, for if he is caught he is dead. He immediately thinks of the Zen temple and its master. He makes all due haste to the temple, and rushes into Bokusan's presence. The samurai is probably dishevelled from the fight; he may even be wounded. Bokusan at once agrees to hide him. I don't know where he puts him – Zen temples are quite spartan, so there can't be many options.

Bokusan goes back to his room. Shortly afterwards, three samurai from the winning side arrive. They have managed to track the fugitive – perhaps they have followed a trail of blood – and they are certain he is somewhere in the temple. They are armed, and their blood is up from the chase, so they do not stand on ceremony. They demand that Bokusan turns their quarry over to them at once. Bokusan calmly replies, 'There's no one here.'

They do not believe him for an instant. They have just been in a fight, they have followed the trail to this place, and they know their enemy is here. They are not prepared to be put off by anybody, not even a Zen master. So they say, 'Right! If you won't tell us, we'll cut off your head.' All three have long sharp swords. Bokusan is unarmed, clad in a simple robe, and unless he leads them to the fugitive they will certainly carry out their threat.

How does he respond? He says, 'Well, if I am to die, I think I'll have a glass of wine.' Going to a little cupboard he takes out a small bottle of wine and a glass. Maybe he was given the wine by one of the temple's supporters for a special occasion and he reckons that his death is a special occasion. In any case, it will be his last chance to taste it.

Bokusan sits down, opens the bottle, and very mindfully, with a steady hand, pours himself some wine – not a big glass, just a small one. He sniffs the wine appreciatively and begins drinking, slowly and happily, savouring each mouthful. 'Mmm, very good....' He becomes totally absorbed in enjoying his glass of wine.

Eventually it is finished. No, he shouldn't really have a second one just because he is going to die – there is no need to get carried away – so he puts down the glass, looks around, and the three men have gone.

The three samurai have been watching this man, whom they have threatened with imminent execution, drinking a glass of wine with total unconcern. He is not engaging with them at all, and they do not know what to do – there is something unnerving about the stillness, the total concentration with which he drinks his wine and savours it. They are nonplussed. Finally they look at one another and leave him unharmed.

*House Styles of Enlightenment*
This is our quite simple story. It is another situation where someone who has been practising Buddhism over many years and has found

freedom through it, faces death. However, Bokusan's response is the complete opposite of Takuan's in the last chapter. Faced with a dangerous situation, Takuan met it head-on. He leapt into the tiger's world, confronted death directly, and made friends with it. Bokusan remains entirely on his own ground, quite unruffled and unconcerned. He does not enter the world of the samurai. He remains aloof like Mount Fuji, so that they cannot get a foothold anywhere. Perhaps if Bokusan had met the tiger, he would have strolled into its cage, sat down with his back to the beast and completely ignored it.

How can we account for these two very different approaches? Anyone who has deep insight into Reality will be unpredictable, because they have broken the grip of habitual tendencies. They are free in each moment, so you cannot predict their actions. This does not mean they are unreliable, it means they are spontaneous, you never quite know where they are going to jump to next because they have such a range of possibilities. Nonetheless, people will still have a style through which they express their insight. This style will depend on their personality and spiritual training. Something we have to take into account when considering the different responses of Takuan and Bokusan is that they come from different schools of Zen Buddhism.

Takuan follows the tradition known as the Rinzai School, which began in ninth-century China. Perhaps its greatest exponent in Japan was Hakuin, who lived in the eighteenth century. Hakuin was an extraordinary person – a painter, calligrapher, and sculptor as well as a great meditator – and he had a very dramatic spiritual life. He claimed he had eighteen major insights into reality, and more minor ones than he could really count. This is in keeping with the whole style of Rinzai Zen – powerful and dramatic. Rinzai himself was the Chinese founder of the school. He used dramatic methods of teaching: shouting, even hitting people, trying to shock them awake from the sleep of ignorance. The Rinzai School became very popular in Japan at the Emperor's court and among the samurai. Its direct, dramatic approach suited men who were regularly faced with life or death situations. The Rinzai School mainly taught through koans, which are existential problems upon which you meditate to take you beyond rational thought to a deeper level of your experience. Knowing something of the Rinzai style, we should not be surprised that Takuan, when asked to meet a tiger, took a strikingly direct approach.

Bokusan, on the other hand, comes from the Sōtō School, the other major school of Zen in Japan. (There is also the Ōbaku School, but that has not been as influential as Sōtō and Rinzai.) Sōtō Zen was brought to Japan by Dōgen (1200–53) and it varies in some respects from the Rinzai approach. Rinzai emphasizes 'sudden enlightenment'. It works to build up pressure: to practise it you need great faith, but also what is known as Great Doubt – an existential question that burns inside you like a molten ball which you can neither swallow down nor vomit up. Rinzai uses meditation on koans to catalyse this experience. Spurred on by the faith that there is an answer which will resolve your existential question, you practise with increasing intensity until you make a breakthrough, like a flash of lightning which illuminates the darkness of your ignorance, and suddenly you see: 'This is how things really are!'

Dōgen's is a more gradual approach. He considered that straining – all this huffing and puffing after Enlightenment – is an expression of one's ego on a more subtle level, strengthening the illusion that there is somewhere to go, something you are going to attain as your possession. So he emphasized what is called *shikan taza* in Japanese, which means 'just sitting'. In meditation, rather than using a koan to break through, you just sit, aware, steady, composed, and contented, and, if there is anything to attain, it matures like a ripening fruit. Dōgen considered that meditating in this aware but purposeless way was itself an expression of your Buddha-nature, your deepest potential. The Sōtō School became the largest Zen tradition in Japan, and it appealed to the common people (for want of a better term), particularly in rural areas.

So perhaps Bokusan, too, responds in the way to which his training has predisposed him: very steady and undramatic, just continuing to pay attention to the details of life. Even when three people say they are going to cut off your head, you calmly carry on, unruffled, unconcerned. There is no reason for any histrionics. If Bokusan is going to die, then he will have a glass of wine. Drinking it is a perfect expression of things as they really are. It is all quite matter of fact.

### Dealing with Information Vacuums

What can we learn, about the human condition and the path to freedom, by putting ourselves into this story? Firstly, what links both Takuan and Bokusan is that, although their responses to crucial situations are very different in expression, they both stay absolutely in the moment, giving themselves up one hundred per cent to the here and now. Takuan leaps completely focused into the tiger's cage. Bokusan pours his glass of wine and then brings all his awareness to the experience, totally absorbed, savouring that drink to the point where the three samurai and their threat have completely disappeared.

Their ability to live in the present frees these men from many of the fears and anxieties that ordinary people suffer. After all, dying is not in the present moment, it is in the future. Whilst it does seem that there can be an instinctive fear, which comes from the body, most fear comes from this tendency to project ourselves into the future, thinking, 'Will I be all right?' or 'What's going to become of me?' This is a constant human tendency. Whilst it is quite natural to wonder what is to become of us, Buddhism – as we have seen – denies that there really is a fixed unchanging self that has gone through all 'our' experiences and whose existence we can project into the future.

Our capacity to imagine the future is a mixed blessing. Employed creatively, it allows us to envision new possibilities, to plan effectively, and to avoid pitfalls. Less positively, it can be used to fill our time with daydreams and fantasies. These are usually a waste of time. We can work against this tendency through practices such as meditation on the breath, which reduce anxiety and tension and strengthen our awareness. But we can also use our ability to project into the future in a way that causes us a great deal of unnecessary suffering. We do this by filling what I call 'information vacuums' with our own imaginings.

For example, sometimes I give series of talks. If there was a good turnout for the first one, as I travel to give the second in the series, I could find myself thinking, 'Well, I wonder how many people there will be? It would really be very embarrassing if after my first talk there were only about five people. It is a sunny day, people may have been hot all day at work or at home, then thinking of the stuffiness of the lecture room they may decide not to come.' I could picture talking to a pitiful handful of bored faces, and make myself miserable. Alternatively, I could imagine that many people appreciated the first talk and will decide to come again so that I shall be addressing a packed room. The reality is that I do not know what is going to happen.

We cannot predict the future, and we human beings usually find this uncertainty very difficult. We find it hard not to fill the vacuum with imaginings, and often what we imagine causes us pain. We may take an exam and then imagine ourselves failing. Indeed, our minds may circle around the topic so that we see ourselves failing this exam over and over again. Then, if we hear we have passed, we realize that we have put ourselves through all that pain completely unnecessarily. Or we may have a child who is taking their exams, and imagine them failing – it is the same process. Or a close friend whom we had arranged to meet at a certain time doesn't turn up. After an hour they have still not appeared and we start thinking they have been run over, or they have deserted us. Or we get a bit of a headache, and if we have a tendency to hypochondria, before we know it we are certain we have a fatal brain tumour.

If we look at the number of times throughout our lives we have put ourselves through the pain of imagining terrible things that never actually happened, because we couldn't bear to leave the vacuum of not knowing unfilled, and then we multiply it by all the billions of people in the world – the total represents a huge mass of completely unnecessary suffering. Surely there is enough actual suffering in life without us multiplying it by needless and painful imaginings. And all this comes about because we cannot just think, 'Well, I don't know what is going to happen.' Therefore it is important to stay alert in situations where there is an information vacuum, and to allow yourself not to know. Or, if that is really asking too much, at least you can practise filling that space with something positive. Imagine your child passing the exam rather than failing. Decide that this headache is really something very minor which will probably clear up by tomorrow rather than the beginning of something terminal!

One of the six main practices of a Bodhisattva is the development of *kṣānti* – patience.[37] An important aspect of patience is accepting the fact that we do not know until we find out. We cannot be sure what the future will bring. We cannot predict when death will come. All we can do is work in the present to set up the best conditions for the future. In particular, we can work to practise the Dharma and follow the path to freedom. If we make efforts now to become more substantial people – more emotionally positive, calm, and energetic – then whatever the future brings we shall have the resources to deal with it.

In Bokusan's position we would cause ourselves a great deal of suffering by leaping off into the future and fearfully imagining the worst, whereas he stays in the present, savouring his glass of wine. He does not send his mind on ahead to imagine what it feels like to be struck by a samurai sword.

### 'Giving Up All Claim on the World'
Naturally, people were very interested in this incident, and Bokusan was often asked about it. Usually he would not discuss it, except on one occasion, when he said

> Well, there is something to be learnt from it. When those fellows came, I did not do what they wanted, but neither did I quarrel with them or plead with them. I just gave up their whole world and had nothing to do with them. And after a time I found they had gone away. Similarly when people complain that they are overwhelmed with passions and wrong thoughts, they should know that the right way is not to quarrel nor to plead or argue. Simply give up all claim on their world and have nothing to do with them, and after a time you will find that they have gone away.[38]

Bokusan here points to two different aspects of freedom, two arenas in which we can practise this 'giving up all claim on the world'. There is freedom in relation to the outside world and other people, which culminates in giving up reliance on the everyday world altogether. Then there is freedom in relation to our own mental states, particularly finding ways of avoiding being overwhelmed by those which are negative. In this section we shall look more generally at what is involved in 'giving up' a 'world'. In the following sections we shall explore it in more practical detail.

To see how we can 'give up all claim on the world', it is important to understand the mechanism by which we steer our way through life. From the raw material of our experience we are all the time selecting certain features on which to concentrate. This happens largely unconsciously, based on our assumptions and preconceptions, as well as our habitual tendencies. Through this process we fashion a 'world' for ourselves. This 'world' is particular to us, though it overlaps with the 'worlds' of other human beings, who are all making their own particular selection from the raw material of experience. Although we have produced it through our choices, the 'world' we live in tends to present itself to us in absolute terms. We experience it as 'how things are'.

Our views and assumptions lead to us 'create a world' because they largely determine the choices we make. Take the example of Paul, a young executive moving quickly up the promotion ladder, who has just got a new job. Driving his workhorse Ford into the car park for a first meeting at his new office, he notices that he is surrounded by Audis, BMWs, and the occasional Mercedes. He soon discovers that cars are important icons of status and success among his new colleagues. Before long he is buried deep in the motoring magazines, quickly followed by a tour of the car dealers to trade in his old Ford, to emerge eventually with something many thousands of pounds more expensive, which allows him to hold up his head in the office car park. Having absorbed his colleagues' values, cars now feature much larger in his world. 'What do you drive?' is a question he often asks new business acquaintances, and to a degree he judges them by their answer. Meanwhile, he is sacrificing other activities in order to save up for something even shinier that will really impress them at work. In this way, Paul starts by changing his views (from seeing cars as useful means of transport to seeing them as status icons). This leads him to make choices in which cars play a much larger part in his world. After a few more years of reading car magazines, and looking at what other people are driving, it feels natural to Paul for cars to be important in this way.

Of course, many of the most enticing world-views are offered to us by people trying to sell us something – be it a new car or an old political ideology. In the case of the latest consumer goodies, quite often they are presented to us as things we must have. How on earth are we going to live without a faster computer, designer label clothes, or whatever it may be? But we can step back from that world-view as it presents itself to us and ask ourselves, 'Do I really need these things (and all those other things that will become future "essentials")?' In buying the latest consumer 'necessity' we are very often not just purchasing an object that will perform a particular function; we are also buying into a view that happiness in life comes from consumerism. Can you really shop your way to freedom?

The consumerist view of the world is relatively easy to see through. It often affects us more by attrition, by sheer weight of numbers – all the advertisements, media images, and so on that we are subjected to in the course of a week – than because the arguments for it are very compelling. However, there are other much deeper views which are harder to see through, particularly if they have been part of our emotional furniture since we were very young. For instance, Paul's girlfriend Vicki was always taught by her mother (from her own bitter experience with her husband) that you cannot trust men. As a result, this has become an article of faith with Vicki, who consequently never feels really secure with Paul. As well as having arguments about the fact that Paul doesn't take her out so often these days because he is saving for a new car, the couple have much more serious rows about the fact that Vicki never trusts Paul when he is out of her sight. Paul has always been faithful, but he feels increasingly caged and restive under Vicki's repeated cross-examinations. As time goes on, tensions around this issue begin to seriously affect their relationship, and Paul eventually finds himself, without quite meaning to, in the arms of a secretary at work. When Vicki finds out, there is an explosion, and she naturally concludes that her mother was right all along.

Most of the filters of views and opinions through which we see the world, and which make things feel 'right' to us come from our conditioning. We have absorbed them from a young age, often by osmosis, from the people around us. Practice of the Dharma is extremely radical, because it involves bringing into sharp awareness the assumptions behind the world-views we were given by our families and schooling – our national, racial, gender, and class backgrounds, as well as those offered us all the time by the media and advertising industries. By challenging all that is false in those assumptions, we can see things in a different way, and begin making new choices. No longer creating a painful or limited world based on an untrue or partial vision of how things are, we move into a world in which we are increasingly free.

This is no easy practice. It requires deep self-knowledge to catch views about ourselves and our life with which we have grown up. It is as if we have been looking at life through spectacles that we never knew we were wearing. Ways of becoming more conscious of these assumptions include meditation (which gives us increased self-awareness), friendship (through which we can have our views and tendencies sympathetically reflected back to us), and the study of the Dharma. Studying Buddhism with other people is particularly effective. Through this we bring our views and ideas into juxtaposition with an Enlightened perspective in a situation in which others can point out to us where we are avoiding or misunderstanding. Through using these methods we gain increasing choice about how to live, and we work to consciously decide the principles on which we wish to base our lives.

To help us develop the clarity to see the assumptions behind what we are usually being offered by our environment, it can be very helpful to give ourselves a respite from it from time to time. This is one of the reasons why Buddhists try to go away regularly on retreat – taking time out to meditate, study the Dharma, and reflect, ideally away from our usual surroundings. As well as giving us a chance to meditate in peaceful conditions, a retreat gives us a chance to look at our experience afresh, to see beyond our current worlds and find new possibilities based on better assumptions.

Whether we are on retreat or not, we need to remain aware, to keep examining the views of life we are being offered by the culture around us, looking at them in the light of our core values. In this way we shall leave behind group values, and become more truly individual – like some great tree growing clear of the forest canopy, stretching up into the sunlight – too big to be used or manipulated.

This is what happened with Bokusan. The samurai assumed they had power over him, that their swords gave them a great deal of negotiating leverage. But Bokusan had left their world behind, he was no longer operating on the same assumptions as they were. So they had no significant power over him, no way of affecting him. He had grown out of their world, in which force was the final arbiter. He had gone beyond being manipulated. His course through life was no longer decided by pleasure or pain, being praised or blamed, gaining or losing, whether he was famous or had a bad reputation. Bokusan had become far too big for the samurai. If he was a tree, their swords would leave barely an impression on his bark.

### Two Different Approaches to Difficulties
Let's look more closely at what this means for us, day to day, in our efforts to move towards freedom. I said that Takuan and Bokusan

were united by the fact that they both stayed aware in the moment. At the same time they do represent two very different approaches in terms of spiritual development. Takuan confronts a problem or a situation head-on, and in a way he represents all those times when we need to do that – when we have to confront the tiger, either within ourselves or in an external situation. Whatever the tiger may be in our own life, we look it straight in the eye.

You can meet situations and people directly; you can confront your own difficulties and negative tendencies head-on. Or you can do the reverse, which is Bokusan's approach. It is almost as if he turns his back on the tiger. He does not put any energy into these three people. As for their threat to cut off his head – he does not give it any time. He does not engage with it at all and, after a while, he finds they have gone away. The Japanese admire courage and a spirit that refuses to bow to circumstance – so they do not carry out their threat.

So we have these two approaches. Sometimes we might confront a situation or difficulty head-on, at other times we might not apply any energy at all and allow it to wither away. We have to be able to use both, skilfully and strategically, as appropriate.

Let's suppose that in meditation one day you are faced with some strong distraction. What can you do about it? There are different approaches you can take. Firstly, you can confront the distraction. You can leave aside the object of your meditation (which you are not concentrating on very well anyway), look objectively at the distraction, and see its consequences. Perhaps you are thinking badly about somebody – think where that could lead. You confront that tendency in yourself – you look at it with a very cool awareness, and you work to change it, to move it on. Secondly, you might decide not to engage with the distraction. To start with, you can try putting more energy into focusing on your concentration-object. If that is unsuccessful, you can adopt what is often called a sky-like attitude – treating the distraction like a cloud passing across the clear blue sky of your mind. The distraction is there like a cloud, but you identify with the broader expanse of your consciousness. Within that broad awareness the cloud of distraction can stay or go as it pleases. You are not caught up with it. You know the distraction is there, but you do not feed it any energy. You give up its world.

Both these approaches can be valid and useful, and it is important to know which to use in a particular situation: whether to confront the tiger, or to leave it alone. How do we decide? The tiger here is a very broad symbol, it might be an aspect of ourselves – difficult feelings or behaviour – or it might be a problem with someone or something outside ourselves.

People like Takuan and Bokusan, men and women who have gained some insight into Reality, act spontaneously. They do not have to work out which approach to take. On another day, if you had asked Takuan to go and see the tiger, he might not have run down to the cage. He might have strolled down there, perhaps eating an apple on the way, and offered the core to the tiger and patted it on the head. Every day would be different. But our spontaneity has not yet arrived at that level, so we need some kind of guideline until we can follow our spiritual intuition completely. There are a few points to be made about this.

### Dustbin Psychology

The first point is that probably, these days, popular psychology weighs quite heavily on the side of confronting the tiger. By popular psychology I mean the kind of amateur psychology that people trade with each other in bars, and during coffee breaks at work. This is often based on a 'Chinese whispers Freudianism' to give a very unsubtle model of how human beings function.[39] At its worst, popular psychology spawns suggestions like the following: You have had various difficult life experiences which have accumulated in your mind like the contents of a dustbin. What you have to do is get your hand right down into the dustbin and pull something out, look at it again, re-experience it, throw it away, and then find another one. Repeat this process, and if you keep going long enough, you will get to the bottom of the dustbin. You will have cleared out everything from the past, and you will feel wonderful.

That is a very crude model of the mind and how to work with it. Certainly, unpleasant incidents have happened to all of us, but for Buddhism a human being is more like an empty stage, on which feelings and actions arise depending on conditions. That does mean that, under the right conditions, certain habitual patterns will be triggered, but it does not imply that there is an irreducible quantity of past difficulties that you have to sift through in order to feel happy.

People who believe in the dustbin model face an impossible task. At times, bringing awareness to past painful events may release energy. But if you keep on focusing attention on those events, you perpetuate them, you set up the conditions for them to continue to arise. Rather than reducing the amount of trash in the dustbin, you can end up reinforcing a pattern of precipitating yourself into painful mental states.

I am not writing off psychology. There are certain painful experiences that have deeply affected people and which they need to explore. But this popular view, which suggests that anything you do not confront is going to fester somewhere in the unconscious depths of your mental dustbin and cause trouble later is not the Buddhist view. I am not advocating repression either. It is obviously not good if something is part of your experience and you unconsciously prevent yourself from experiencing it. However, you do not have to go to the other extreme and explore all the psychological ramifications of your difficulties or problems. Sometimes you can just let them go.

Popular psychology is overweighting the balance in favour of Takuan's approach – scaring us with the idea that if we do not confront the tiger, there will be trouble. But the tiger of the emotions is not a real tiger which is constantly lurking, waiting to cause trouble unless we confront it. Rather it is a dream tiger, that only arises in dependence upon certain conditions.

### Changing the Problem by Changing Your Level of Consciousness
Bokusan adopts a different kind of approach to his situation. He deals with it by changing levels. The samurai are trying to corner him by saying, 'Either you give up this fugitive, or we cut off your head.' In response, Bokusan does not operate on their level. Instead, he moves into a world of aesthetic appreciation. It is not high-level aesthetic appreciation, it is a glass of wine, but it is still aesthetic appreciation. They are trying to manipulate him to do something – he just does not play.

The point that I want to make here is that changing your level of consciousness is doing something about the problem or situation. We have all had the experience of trying to do some work when we are a bit tired and irritable. Maybe you are working with a computer, trying to get something done, and because you are tired you do not make a very good job of it. It all takes far longer than it ought to, and actually the best thing to do would be to stop, go for a walk or have a cup of tea, and come back refreshed. You would then solve your problem more easily. Plodding on in your current state of mind is a very ineffective way of trying to solve a problem. In fact, it can become counterproductive. This kind of everyday experience demonstrates that even a little change of consciousness can make a difference to a problem. A major shift of consciousness, such as one can make if one meditates regularly and practises the Dharma, can make a radical difference.

Because we often tend to think of our problems and difficulties as something given, they become absolute. When we are in them, that is how they are, that is how we are. But if we change our level of consciousness we change the context, therefore we change the problem. It is a bit like a house with a number of floors. If you move up a floor there is different furniture. If you raise your level of consciousness then your mental furniture may still be reminiscent of the lower levels, but it is brighter and there is more space around it.

If you observe yourself closely, you will notice that there are some problems and difficulties that dominate your thinking when you are on a certain level of consciousness which do not seem to be there when you are in a better state. Perhaps you go on retreat and practise more meditation than usual. In doing so, you transcend your previous level of consciousness. In that higher state the problem vanishes. ('Oh that, yes, I was worried about that before I went on retreat wasn't I?') People like Bokusan and Takuan have changed levels so drastically, up to the level of transcendental insight, that even the problem of birth and death has vanished without trace.

Sometimes, rather than banging our heads against some intractable aspect of ourselves, or some seemingly insoluble problem, we would do best to change the context. In particular, we can try to expand our awareness. The problem may not go away, but it will be much easier to resolve on a different level.

It can be useful in this regard to make a distinction between 'difficulties' and 'problems'. A 'difficulty', in the sense I am using it here, is something that can be solved on its own level, whereas a 'problem' cannot. A problem, defined in this way, requires a shift of consciousness, a change of context before it can be solved.

Sometimes people will present you with dilemmas that are insoluble on their own terms. On the level of their dilemma it is as if there is furniture everywhere, one piece piled on another, with everything crammed so closely together that it could never be disentangled and there is no room for manoeuvre. There is no solution on the level on which the issue is being presented. You can spend hours talking to someone about such a problem, and by the end they are often very pleased and grateful to you for spending so much time discussing what to do – but nothing has actually changed. Rather than relating to someone on the basis of their problems, it is often better to try to widen their emotional horizons by affirming the healthier parts of their experience.

### Facing the Tiger, or Leaving it Alone

If we bear these points in mind, we shall be in a better position to decide between our two strategies – facing the tiger or leaving it alone. As usual in Buddhism, the decision depends on our motivation. Why do we want to confront this particular tiger?

We might want to do so for quite negative reasons. For instance, we might be too anxious or impatient to be able to let things be. Sometimes people can be very decisive for the wrong reasons. I have been in groups where we were wondering what to do about some matter, and someone would say very definitely, 'Oh yes, we need to do this, this, and this.' Everyone else, impressed with the confidence of their assertion, would go along with it. Later it turned out that their confident proposals were completely wrong, and I was left wondering, 'How come they seemed so certain about it?' People sometimes act in this way because they cannot bear not knowing what to do. Rather than living with the uncertainty they clutch at the first solution that occurs to them. This often looks like real leadership and decisiveness, but it has actually come out of 'I can't stand this, let's *do something*!' Confronting the tiger on that basis will not be very useful or effective.

Alternatively, facing the tiger could be based on positive mental states. For instance, it could arise out of care for someone. There could be a situation in which you feel great concern for a friend, so you leap in and meet them, engaging them with all the energy you have available. Or it could come from a desire to make a positive change in yourself, to resolve something which really does need resolving.

We have to be aware and honest with ourselves. What is our motivation? Why are we putting energy into this situation? Are we acting out of anxiety or restlessness, or from a genuine desire to make a difference?

The same questions apply to deciding to give up the tiger's world. We may be holding back out of fear or a sort of aloof pride, or from lack of concern we may have created what a friend of mine once called a 'somebody else's problem field': 'Look! That tiger is about to break out of its cage. Somebody ought to do something about it....' We keep our distance, not wanting to become involved. Many people in the West like to look 'cool' and detached, and score points with their friends for doing so, but this often means they are not really engaging with life.

We may also decide – from very positive motives – that we will not put energy into some situation. We may think the best way to resolve some negative aspect of ourselves is to starve it of energy, widen our sphere of interest, and grow beyond the problem. If we grow beyond it, it will become smaller in relation to the rest of us, so we may decide quite positively to change the problem by changing the level or the context in which we face it.

We need to be careful when taking decisions of this kind. It is not as if there is an absolute rule: 'Always do this, always do that.' No one can provide us with that. It is one of those aspects of the path to freedom with which we need to experiment to see what works, and to learn from our mistakes. It also helps if we can become aware of our habitual tendencies. Some people habitually avoid. They keep their options open because of an underlying fear or lack of engagement. Others habitually confront, out of tension, their inability to let things rest.

Whatever we do – whether we decide to face the tiger or leave it alone – we must do it wholeheartedly. For instance, if we have tried unsuccessfully to give up the tiger's world, then we should resolutely engage with it. The main thing, as a Zen saying goes, is 'don't wobble'.

### Is the Zen Master a Liar and a Drunkard?

We have now explored some of the lessons of our story, but there may be a couple of doubts about Bokusan lingering in your mind which I had better try to dispel. To put it bluntly – in facing the tiger style – is he a liar, and a drunkard?

When the three samurai claim he is hiding a fugitive, Bokusan says, 'There's no one here.' Isn't that a lie? Now you could argue that he is only telling a white lie in order to save someone's life, which is a reasonable thing to do. But in a way he is not lying at all. He is talking on another level of truth, from the viewpoint of ultimate Reality on which there are no fixed unchanging entities, just a flow of different processes. So from that understanding, when Bokusan says, 'There's no one here,' it is true. However, it is a truth that the three samurai cannot understand.

What about that glass of wine? The fifth of the basic Buddhist precepts is to abstain from intoxicants that dull the mind. In addition, the moment of death is considered by most Buddhist traditions a crucial time at which to remain aware. So why does Bokusan want to drink wine and cloud his awareness when he is facing death? It must be said that Buddhists interpret the fifth precept in different ways. Some take it that you should never take any drink or drugs that cloud the mind – except where really necessary for medical reasons. Others consider it okay to take the occasional glass of something, provided you do not become unmindful. Unfortunately, some Buddhist teachers in the West have themselves fallen prey to drink, and have sometimes even tried to rationalize their actions in terms of the Dharma. Even if they themselves are not affected adversely by their alcohol consumption (which is, frankly, unlikely) we who are not that spiritually developed should not be trying to emulate them in this regard. The path to freedom involves maintaining as much awareness as possible in all situations. The use of drink and drugs defeats that purpose. If after we have had a drink or two we are not fit to be in charge of a car, we are also not fit to be in charge of our minds, which from the point of view of our quest for freedom is the most vital requirement of all. So if we are going to drink or take drugs socially, we have to be very honest with ourselves about the effect they have on our consciousness.

We also have to take into account the fact that, in the case of alcohol and other drugs, we are supporting a multimillion-pound industry that produces a vast number of alcoholics and drug addicts. Even when people are not actually alcoholic, heavy drinking has many negative consequences for our health. Experts estimate that alcohol is a factor in one-third of all hospital admissions in the UK. Even if we are certain we shall not fall into such states, do we really want to give our money to organizations that are implicated in creating so much suffering? (In the next chapter we shall see an example of the trouble drink can cause when we have to deal with a drunken samurai.)

But perhaps we should not become too concerned about Bokusan having a drink at this point. After all, he is a realized Buddhist master, and presumably he is not drinking the wine for its effect on his mind. He wants to savour something in what may be the last moments of his life, before disappearing from this level of experience. It is quite extraordinary that he is not drinking to summon up Dutch courage. He is doing it for some aesthetic enjoyment – admittedly on rather a low level.

That was our 'small glass of wine', which can give us a taste of some new possibilities: of living in the moment, and not filling information vacuums with fears, anxieties, and negative thoughts; of not accepting the world on its own terms, but growing beyond it through awareness, through practice of the Dharma, until at last we are too big to be used or manipulated; of the development of awareness, so that we can either fully confront things or leave them completely alone, changing the problem by changing the context, particularly by changing our level of consciousness. It can give us a taste of what it would be like to pour ourselves into meditation, into practising the Dharma, so deeply, enjoying it so much, concentrating so strongly, that we finally reach a point where all our worries and troubles, all our fears, even our fear of death, have gone away.

This is not simply a story of patience and unruffled equanimity. Nor is it only a story of deep concentration, although Bokusan does become totally immersed (not literally!) in his glass of wine. It is not even just a story about insight that goes beyond life and death. It is a true story of deep compassion, for Bokusan has risked his life to save the hidden fugitive. Presumably the man is hiding somewhere in the temple, listening for the sound of his three pursuers coming to hunt him out. However, instead of the samurai he hears the soft padding of Bokusan's straw sandals coming to tell him the coast is clear. Perhaps after the fugitive's frightening wait he will be in need of a glass of wine....

# What Shall We Do with the Drunken Samurai?

### The Teacher of Emperors

I spent part of the summer of 1980 on the Greek islands. One of the things I enjoyed most was being ferried around – sometimes in small fishing boats, sometimes in larger vessels – from one island to another. I have vivid memories of taking an overnight boat to Thira, spending the voyage on deck looking up at the stars in the Mediterranean sky whilst all the Greeks were down in the stuffy saloon watching Benny Hill on television. One of my journeys took me to the island of Sifnos, where the sea was so rough that the ferry had difficulty berthing. Those of us waiting to disembark crowded into the exit area while the captain, resplendent in yards of gold braid, directed operations, trying to lower the ramp at the front of the boat. There were very few tourists, just one or two backpackers. The crowd consisted mainly of local people, including women with chickens and goats. It was a very tricky operation stabilizing the ramp. Every now and then it would crash on to the quay and people would surge forward hopefully. Then the ship would heave, the captain would speak urgently into his intercom, the ramp would start rising again, and a tide of people, goats, and chickens would ebb back into the boat.

I remembered my Greek travels when I was thinking about this chapter, because in this third story from *The Tiger's Cave* we shall be taking a ferry trip.[40] On board we shall meet the drunken samurai of the title of this chapter. In my (very associative) mind, a combination of boats and the drunken samurai reminded me of that sea shanty.

In Chapter 1 we accompanied Donald Crowhurst in his small boat on the long journey into the South Atlantic and back, until finally he kept an appointment with Death. In this last chapter, as we board another boat, it may feel as though we have come full circle, particularly as once again it seems that one of the passengers has an appointment with the man with the scythe. However, whereas Crowhurst was like the Ancient Mariner,

> *Alone, alone, all, all alone,*
> *Alone on a wide wide sea!*

the ferry includes a Zen master among its passengers, so we can have some hope that all will turn out well.

For this story we go back roughly 650 years to fourteenth-century Japan. The hero of our story is another Zen master. This one is called Musō Kokushi or Musō Soseki, and he was born in 1275, and is destined to die in 1351. He would probably not be bothered if you had told him. He is not concerned about the future. His mind is happily wedded to the present moment.[41]

Musō is a courteous and cultured person, descended from an aristocratic family. He became a monk at an early age, as it was common practice for noble families to offer a child to become a monk. As a monk he naturally practised meditation, but he was also very interested in the arts and literature, and managed to combine a large literary output with a great deal of spiritual teaching.

Musō became renowned both as a poet – particularly in a poetic form known as *tanka*, a kind of short song – and as a great artist in the genre called *sumi*. Sumi is Japanese painting executed with black Chinese ink and brushes, which can produce very varied effects because the ink can be applied thickly or very lightly. It was quite a while before Musō's main Zen teacher, Kōhō, acknowledged him as a Zen master. Koho probably thought Musō was spending too much time reading and writing, when Kōhō would rather have seen him meditating. So Musō had to spend a long time meditating in seclusion before Kōhō would authorize him to teach.

Having gained that sanction, Musō went on to became the teacher of emperors and shōguns. He had free access to both the Imperial Court and the Shōgunate, and was celebrated as much for his painting and writing as for his spiritual qualities. He also produced more than fifty disciples who gained insight into Reality.

*An Overloaded Ferry*

Musō must have been fairly old by the time of this incident, because naturally it takes a while to become teacher to the Emperor. As our story begins, he is on a journey. I do not know where he is coming from or going to. (If you ask a Zen master that, I suspect you will get a paradoxical answer!) Accompanying him is a friend and Zen student of his who also happens to be an expert swordsman. At a certain point in their journey the two friends come to a river that can be crossed only by ferry.

Ferries are important in myth and legend, because very often they take you across from one land to another. Sometimes they take you from the land of the living to the land of the dead, as in Greek myth or in D.H. Lawrence's 'The Ship of Death'. In Buddhism, ferries have mythic significance because the 'other shore' in Buddhism is a symbol for the world of freedom, Nirvāṇa. At present we are in saṁsāra, the world of unsatisfactoriness, in which we are subject to old age, sickness, death, being parted from what we like, etc. As we saw in Chapter 6, the Buddha once described the Dharma as being like a raft, which takes us from this shore of unsatisfactoriness to that other shore, the world of permanent freedom, peace, and so forth. So for a Buddhist and poet like Musō the ferry would naturally have an archetypal resonance, as he waits to board. The ferry of course has a ferryman, who is filling his vessel with passengers. Musō climbs aboard, and his friend takes all their baggage and sits on the opposite side of the boat.

A fourteenth-century Japanese ferry is unlikely to be very large or perhaps very stable. There is still a crowd of people waiting to board with their luggage. The ferryman makes a charge, and naturally tries to cram in as many people as he possibly can, until it can hold no more. It is like ferries one can still find nowadays in India, weighed down with as many people as they can possibly carry, and then a few more! Finally the boatman decides he really cannot take any more passengers, and starts turning people away. He is about to cast off when barging his way through the crowd comes a samurai. He comes up to the ferryman, who can smell his breath – which is afire with alcohol.

We do not know what time of day this is. If it is 'early in the morning' (as in the eponymous sea shanty) then this already-intoxicated samurai has a bad problem. All we know is that he is drunk, and he wants to cross the river now. He is not waiting for the next boat, and he will not be turned away by any fool of a ferryman.

What is the ferryman to do? There is only one thing he can do in his position. He is just an ordinary man, trying to make a living. He does not have the power to confront this drunken warrior with his sword. So, hardly pausing to think, he allows the samurai on board. Naturally, he is worried about allowing a heavily-weighted drunk on his already full vessel, but he does what many of us do. We just hope things will turn out all right. We ignore something, telling ourselves it will be okay and we shall probably get away with it. And we do get away with it, most of the time....

The ferryman casts off, and the boat starts to cross the river, which is quite broad. The samurai is not only drunk, he is in a bad mood. Maybe he has been drinking out of frustration. Perhaps there is some deep unhappiness in him, and he drinks to cover that up. Whatever the reason, he soon starts a quarrel. We are not told the reason for the dispute. Perhaps he is arguing with the ferryman over the fare. He is standing up, swaying about unsteadily, and making himself unpleasant. Not only that, the boat is beginning to rock and is very low in the water. If the samurai continues this behaviour he may capsize it.

Musō is sitting there, crammed in among the crowd. Everyone is aware of what is going on, but they are completely quiet, like people on the London Underground when there is an unpleasant incident, all gazing fixedly at the advertisements or at the floor. But Musō is not like that. He is keenly aware what is going on. He knows very well that actions have consequences, that even people's mental states have consequences. He sees that unless something is done the boat will capsize. So he speaks up.

Musō intervenes in a civil manner. After all, he comes from an aristocratic family, and is very cultured. He politely points out to the samurai that if he does not sit down the boat might sink, and they could all drown. (The samurai, with his heavy sword, is likely to be first to reach the bottom of the river.)

Now the samurai is drunk, and he does not like being told what to do at the best of times. He is certainly not going to lose face by sitting down because he is asked to do so by some interfering, shaven-headed so-and-so. Not only does he have his sword, he also has an iron war fan in his hand, a very solid implement. The samurai lurches over to where Musō is sitting, crying 'Meddling priest!' and lashes out with his fan.

There are many stories of Zen masters who are resourceful and spontaneous in the face of unexpected danger. I remember reading an account by Alan Watts of two Americans who went to visit a Zen master. They had decided beforehand to test him by trying to catch him off guard. One of them had a paper fan, and in the middle of their conversation he suddenly threw it at the Zen master. The master ducked sharply in mid-sentence, and the fan went straight through the paper screen behind him.

However, Zen masters are not magicians. Musō is wedged in among the crowd. He has no alternative but to take the blow. The iron fan hits him on the forehead. Musō does nothing in response. He just sits there with blood trickling into his eyes.

Striking out has the effect of releasing something in the samurai. Sometimes, when someone is feeling frustrated and angry and trying to pick a quarrel they are really trying to 'meet' somebody. They are trying to find something solid, to gain some sense of who they are by bumping up against someone else. Now the samurai has discharged some emotion and is satisfied. He has silenced the impudent priest and put him in his place, so he slumps down in the boat (there is not really space to slump down, but people somehow make room) and does not cause any more trouble.

Musō of course is not alone; he has a friend with him. This man, we know, is an expert swordsman. He too is wedged within the crowd, and can do nothing to prevent Musō from being struck. He is frustrated and very angry that this drunk has struck his friend, who also happens to be the Zen teacher of the Emperor and the Shōgun. So he sits, dwelling darkly on what has happened, waiting for the boat to reach dry land so he can settle the score with the samurai. There is a charged, unnaturally quiet atmosphere on the boat as it makes the long crossing. It finally arrives at the bank of the river and disgorges its passengers on the shore.

The samurai has been half asleep, but as people begin to disembark he starts up. He then registers, from a few words exchanged between them, that Musō has a friend with him who is armed. Suddenly aware that there may be repercussions from lashing out with his fan, he looks threateningly at Musō's companion, who gazes coolly back at him. This worries the samurai a little, and he watches appraisingly to see how the man moves as he disembarks. Musō's friend picks up the bags, leaps lightly ashore, deposits the luggage carefully on the ground, checks his sword, and stands in the path of the samurai, who is weaving unsteadily off the ferry. There is going to be a duel.

If you have practised swordsmanship yourself, you can tell an expert swordsman by the way he moves and stands. There is a balance, a centredness, a lightness and alertness which you can recognize. On the ferry the drunk had realized that he might be in for a fight. Now, watching Musō's friend take his stand, the samurai is experienced enough to know that he is not in for a fight; he is in for a defeat. Who would have thought it? This river-bank is where he is going to meet his end. He has been ferried across to the land of the dead.

Probably none of us can tell where we shall breathe our last, but the samurai now knows the time and the place where death will claim him. Miserably defiant, he prepares himself to take his final stand, with a hangover. He may tell himself that if he had a clear head, he would stand a chance. He would be wrong. He has no chance. He has nothing of Musō's friend's skill, speed, timing, and courage. So he takes his useless stand on the shore, facing his unwavering opponent.

They eye one another. The drunk prepares to make the first move. It offers him no hope, but it is better than being cut down in useless defence. The expert watches, taking in his opponent's eyes, posture, and breathing pattern, which all provide tell-tale signs of the lunging attack that will be effortlessly parried. The drunk will probably not even see the deadly riposte that will follow it.

The drunk's knuckles tighten on his sword. Subtle tensing of muscles telegraphs his coming attack. And at that moment Musō jumps forward, with a great cry of 'No!' It is like watching Takuan leap into the tiger's cage, holding nothing back. Musō sees what is happening, and intervenes without hesitation. The two protagonists, caught at the last instant, draw back a little, still eyeing each other. Musō turns to his friend, who is waiting for his moment with the drunken samurai, and says, 'Now, now is the time to apply our Buddhism. These forms are emptiness. Anger and all the passions are the Bodhi.' Then he quietly takes his friend by the shoulder and leads him away.

## The Samurai's Response

Here our story ends, although one could wish to know much more. It would be interesting to find out how the participants responded after this incident. Did Musō's friend allow himself to be led away out of respect for his teacher? Or did Musō's graphic demonstration of non-retaliation bring home to him that 'hatred does not cease by hatred; hatred ceases only by love'?

What about the drunken samurai? He had thought he was going to die on the bank of that river. Did he thank his lucky stars that he had survived? Or after a while did he kid himself that he would have won the duel, that the Zen priest gave his opponent an excuse to back out of a contest he could not win? Or is it possible that as a result of this incident the samurai changed his life? Did he feel gratitude to Musō for showing compassion to him and saving him from certain death? After all, Musō didn't owe him any favours after that blow from the iron fan. Or did something of the samurai's frustration disappear as a result of having at last met someone who was worthy of respect, someone who actually embodied a higher and more fulfilling way of life?

I answer many questions at Buddhist centres. People often ask interesting questions; occasionally they persist with awkward, aggressive questions. When this happened I used to wonder, 'What are they here for? If they really think Buddhism is such a waste of time, and they are so suspicious of it, why do they bother with it?' But I have realized over the years that actually such people are often very idealistic. They have a sense of something higher, and they have tried to find it in one situation after another, only to be let down. So they ask challenging questions to test you to see whether you are genuine. Do you really know, or are you just producing fancy ideas? It is possible that the frustrated samurai recognizes that he has at last met someone who can give meaning to his life. Does he later find out that he has struck the teacher of his emperor with his war fan? Does he feel remorse for that? We cannot know. We can only put ourselves into the story imaginatively and see what *our* drunken samurai does and how he feels.

A point in the samurai's favour is that he did what Musō asked. He did stop rocking the boat, and sat down quietly. But initially he reacted angrily, as people often do when criticized. If we care deeply about our friends, there will be times when we shall feel the need to challenge or criticize something about them which is limiting or unhelpful to them. Even when we do this very carefully and kindly they do not often reply, 'Thank you very much. I hadn't realized that I was falling so far short in this area. I am very pleased that you have pointed it out to me.' Naturally enough, they react with anger or defensiveness. I am not condoning it. They shouldn't do it. It will only cause them suffering and trouble. But very often this is what human beings do.

If we are trying to point out something to someone and they do react in this way, it really does not help if we then say, 'Look, now you are reacting negatively. You are being very sensitive about this.' If someone does take it badly when we point something out to them, we need to try to convince them that we care about them and that is why we are being critical. We have taken the trouble to challenge them because we feel there is something they are doing which really is not helping them – which is causing, or likely to cause, suffering to themselves or others. If we keep expressing care and concern in this way, then usually – after a while – we can convince our friend that we are not attacking them but trying to help.

### Dwelling in the Gap

For me the main message to be drawn from this story is one that underlies all the freedom stories in this book, and relates particularly closely to the material on reciprocal relationships in Chapter 4. It is something which I could (and may well) write a whole book about. Let's leave aside the specific personalities and details of this incident, and look at the underlying issues. We shall look at three parts of the story in turn.

First, there is the incident on the ferry, when Musō speaks up, asking the samurai to be careful not to sink the boat, and the samurai's angry riposte. Why does the samurai respond violently? If we were able to analyse what happened inside him, we should find something like the following chain of internal events. (The sequence would probably be a little blurred, because the sake, or whatever it is that the samurai has been drinking, is affecting all his functions.) First the Zen master's words would impinge on the samurai's ears, and the message would produce in him painful feelings. These would be immediately followed by concepts, perhaps a little jumbled by drink, amounting to the fact that the priest is telling him what to do in front of the crowd of passengers. As a result, there arises in the samurai a desire, akin to that of a wounded animal, to put an end to the pain the situation is causing him.

(It may even be that unconsciously the samurai responds to the kindness in Musō's tone. The samurai is probably used to people talking to him with fear in their voices, or with command or contempt. To be spoken to with kindness and civility may, strangely enough, provoke in him a deeper pain – the pain of his estrangement from friendship and human warmth. This may be the deeper goad that causes him to lash out.)

Driven by the desire to put an end to the painful feeling he is experiencing, the samurai, out of control, moves across the boat and deals Musō that blow. If we were to summarize in the simplest way what has happened, we could say that the samurai reacted automatically to a painful stimulus.

As so often in life, an action by which one person salves their pain becomes a source of suffering for someone else. Of course the blow is painful for Musō, but for the moment I am more concerned with Musō's friend. The sight of the iron fan striking his teacher's forehead produces some very painful feelings in him. However, he cannot respond immediately (at least not without risking a fracas that will sink the boat). He has the rest of the journey in which to dwell on how to respond to that painful event. The more he dwells on it, and the more reasons he gives himself for anger at the samurai's action, the stronger his own painful emotions become. Musō is his great friend and teacher, to whom he is devoted. It is painful to see someone you love treated so violently. Doubtless he dwells on the injustice of the samurai's action. Then there are issues of status. Musō is a magnificent teacher, a great man, revered by shōgun and emperor, and this drunken fool has had the temerity to strike him. Musō's friend may also feel a certain irrational guilt. As well as being a companion to Musō on their journey, he may also have taken upon himself the role of bodyguard. He may reproach himself for not having placed himself in a position to intervene. Powerlessness and frustration add to his pain, and stoke the anger and desire for revenge that he feels.

Thus Musō's companion experiences a toxic brew of painful feelings. Naturally he wants to put an end to them, which manifests as the desire to fight a duel with the samurai. In fact, to talk of duelling is to dignify what is to happen. Under the warrior code of Japanese society it may be legitimate to challenge someone in this way. However, the expert with the sword must know that there can only be one outcome to challenging someone who is only a mediocre swordsman, and whose reactions are affected by alcohol. Whilst it may be dignified by being called a duel, it is really premeditated murder. So if we analyse what goes on in Musō's companion, we find that in response to a painful stimulus he dwells on a response, but the response is conditioned by, and on the same violent level as, the stimulus.

Moving forward again, we come to the point in the story when victim and executioner are facing one another on the river bank. The painful sequence of events is about to reach its inevitable conclusion when Musō quickly intervenes. Musō too has had a painful stimulus to respond to – that blow to the head. But he has developed spiritually to the point where he does not respond automatically to such things. In response to being given a bloody head, he saves the samurai's life.

We could look at this scene on the river bank symbolically. The samurai stands for the painful stimuli in our lives to which we habitually react. Musō's friend represents our habitual reaction, conditioned by the stimulus. If this process follows its course, an automatic response will occur, which will then lead to more pain and suffering. We can only break this chain by introducing more awareness into the situation. Musō here stands for the consciousness that we can create in ourselves through Buddhist practice, an ethical and compassionate awareness that is not conditioned by stimuli, but which responds creatively, introducing a new and higher element into the situation.

The whole path to freedom relies on creating a gap of awareness between stimulus and response. In the story of Musō and the samurai, the stimuli are painful, but this point also holds good when we are confronted with stimuli that create pleasurable responses within us; here too we have to create a gap of awareness so that we are not overwhelmed by pleasurable sensations and react automatically. In that gap we can find the most creative response, which may be to go along with what the stimulus is spurring us to do, or not. On a summer's day, the pleasure of the sunlight streaming through our window may urge us outside, and after creating that gap of awareness we may follow its prompting to walk in the park. However, there may be other pleasurable stimuli – the banoffi pie of which we have already had two helpings, or our wife's best friend looking particularly attractive today – which we shall be aware enough to resist.

It is no exaggeration to say that our freedom as human beings depends on creating a gap of awareness between feeling and response. As long as we are led by the nose – by pleasurable feeling exciting our craving, and painful feeling stinging us to fear or aggression – we shall never be free. We could have the perfect house, the ideal partner, and a massive fortune, and still have no freedom at all. However, if we could create a strong enough awareness, wise and compassionate, we could be bound hand and foot in solitary confinement and still have our freedom.

Having intervened, Musō says to his friend, 'Now, now is the time to apply our Buddhism.' Creating the gap of awareness between stimulus and response requires us to stay awake, to be alive to what is going on in the present moment. Now, in this very moment, is the time to apply our Buddhism, to follow the path to freedom, by maintaining awareness between each stimulus and our response to it, and not being dictated to by pleasure or pain, or any of the other worldly winds. Whatever life brings us, we aim to respond creatively, with loving-kindness. As we continue doing this we shall feel our freedom growing, along with a sense of deep equanimity and peace that cannot be shaken by the ups and downs of everyday life.

### Taking Buddhism to Heart

In particular, the time to apply our Buddhism is when things are going badly for us. There are times when it is quite easy to practise the Dharma. We can usually do it when we have the right conditions – at a Buddhist centre, or on retreat in the country; we remember to practise the precepts, to be aware, to practise loving-kindness. But we really need to remember the Dharma when the going gets tough, when times are hard, when we are feeling near the end of our tether, and when life is not being fair.

I have worked in several Buddhist centres over the years. One thing that is noticeable is how newer people regularly come along when they are in fairly good states, but disappear for a while when they are going through a difficult patch. Perhaps something goes wrong in their lives, or they are upset about something, and they decide not to come to the centre for a while, and to stop seeing their Buddhist friends. Sometimes they do this because they do not want to trouble their friends, or to be a long face around the centre. Very often they do it in order to maintain an image of themselves as happy and okay. So when they are not in those states they vanish for a couple of weeks (or however long it takes until they feel better) and then start coming along again.

It is a great pity when people disappear in this way. Often you make a real breakthrough when you do not feel good – perhaps feel at your worst – and you manage to turn to the Dharma, and in particular to your spiritual friends. When you are feeling low is the time you discover that you can rely on the Dharma and on the sangha – on other people who are practising loving-kindness, compassion, and so forth.

This means we need to make the most of the opportunity when times are not too hard and we have good conditions. Studying the Dharma, meditating, and making deep friendships with like-minded people, will give us the momentum to see us through times when life becomes difficult. Then, when we are faced with one of our own personal tigers, we shall naturally turn to the Dharma and to our spiritual friends.

'Applying our Buddhism' in difficult situations includes remembering that life is not fair. This has been well demonstrated by what has happened to our three Zen masters. Takuan, after all, does not do anything to deserve having to face a Korean tiger. He is sitting in the sunshine minding his own business, when the Shōgun says, 'Does Zen have anything else to show us?' Bokusan hides a fugitive out of compassion, and as a result three armed men threaten to decapitate him. Musō just points out, in a polite way, that the drunken samurai may drown himself and everyone else. All he receives for his concern is 'Meddling priest!' and a blow on the forehead. Nobody promised you that life would be fair. If they did, they lied. At times when life is being unfair we can remember the Dharma, reminding ourselves that saṁsāra is unreliable. We can be sure that it will end in tears, one way or another, because it is impermanent and unsatisfactory.

## Ways of Working with Raw Emotions

These three Zen stories have given us keys to ways in which we can work on our own raw, unrefined feelings and volitions. We saw the swordsman Yagyū facing that tiger – representing those instinctual forces in ourselves – and holding them in check by force of will. Sometimes we may have to do that with our own raw energies; if we do not, they may burst out and hurt somebody. Meditation and Dharma practice tend to increase our energy, and put us in deepening contact with our emotions. Learning the art of emotional containment is a vital aspect of spiritual life. At times one has to hold one's emotions, not giving them expression but containing them within the crucible of one's awareness until they have been transformed.

Takuan demonstrates the final resolution of the conflict between spiritual aspiration and unrefined emotion. He is not afraid of these strong energies; in fact he is quite at home with them. He speaks their language: spitting on his hand, so that the tiger licks it. He meets the tiger on its level and makes friends with it. If we are to succeed on the path to freedom we need to develop loving-kindness for ourselves on a deep level; we have to become a friend to all aspects of ourselves. This does not mean accepting ourselves uncritically, thinking that how we are 'warts and all' is okay. We really work to transform ourselves, but we do it on the basis of friendliness and acknowledging what is there, in order to be able to transform it. Takuan 'tames' the tiger by establishing friendly communication with it.

In the second story it is the three samurai who represent the more instinctual forces in ourselves. Bokusan's approach is not to engage energy with these forces on their own level. He continues mindfully dwelling in states of aesthetic appreciation. He does not set up the conditions in which these forces can come into play negatively.

What is Musō's approach in the third story? It is summed up by what he says to his friend when he leads him away. First he says, 'These forms are emptiness.' Musō is reminding his disciple that this samurai is just a process, in constant flux – sometimes drunk, sometimes sober – of continuous change on all levels. Life is a flow, a process arising in dependence on conditions. What we are angry with, what we identify as the cause of our problems in life, finally has no inherent existence. This means that, ultimately, there is no samurai to be upset about. Challenging him to a duel is on the deepest level 'a dialogue in a dream' – which, incidentally, is the name of one of Musō's most famous works.[42]

Musō's approach may be hard for us to use. We shall need to have quite a strong grasp on the Buddhist view of Reality before we can employ it successfully in confronting our own negative states. It is important to understand it, however, and when we have travelled some way down the path to freedom we shall find that this approach is the most effective antidote to any trouble or suffering.

Not only does Musō say that all forms are emptiness; he also says, 'Anger and all the passions are the Bodhi.' Bodhi means 'illumination' – it is a word for Enlightenment. This is quite a strange idea: that anger and all the passions are illumination, Enlightenment. It does not mean that everything is one, that we are all Enlightened anyway so it doesn't matter what we do! Enlightenment is a state of permanent satisfaction, happiness, and bliss, and when we allow ourselves to become furiously angry with someone, or very resentful, we do not feel very blissful!

There are three ways in which we can look at what Musō is saying here. The first is that he could be pointing out to his friend that the whole of life, including this drunken bully, is a manifestation of Reality. The drunken samurai is a perfect example of the way in which everything arises in dependence upon conditions. Another, perhaps more useful, way of looking at it is that all the passions are expressions of energy. Musō's friend is very angry with the samurai, and as a result is in a highly-charged state. Having large amounts of energy is in itself a good thing. The problem is to prevent it being expressed destructively, and to find channels for it that take us towards freedom. The challenge usually is to 'unhook' the energy from the object with which it has become caught up. Let's imagine that Musō leads his friend away from the river-bank and they find a quiet place in which to sit and meditate. Musō's friend's blood is still boiling, but he follows his teacher's injunction. He works to let go of the incident of the samurai. Having unhooked his feelings from their object, he now experiences the anger simply as very strong waves of energy flowing through his body.

This 'unhooking' of the energy can be used whenever we are caught up in high-energy negative states, whether of anger, craving, or jealousy. At first it can take a considerable effort of will to let drop our intense involvement with the object, but if we manage to do so, and to own the energy, we can find ourselves in some very positive and liberated states indeed. With deeper practice we can even take the process a stage further. As well as unhooking from the object, we can also unhook from the subject, letting go of the idea that 'I' am experiencing the energy. Finally we are left with experiences of pure energy. At this stage we shall be able to feel for ourselves how the passions, 'unhooked' in this way, can be expressions of Enlightenment.

A third possible interpretation of Musō's injunction is that all our feelings, including anger, hurt, greed, jealousy, fear, and so on, have no absolute validity. Our mental states quite often present themselves to us as if they are absolute. If we are feeling depressed, say, it is hard for us to remember feeling any other way. We also tend to think that our view of life from that mental state is absolute: 'This is how the world is.' We do not realize that we are filtering our experience through our current mood and view of life, both of which are partial and changing. In any strong negative state, it is very hard to conceive of things being different. (One of the ways in which one can recognize negative states is by their inflexibility.) But what Musō is saying is that these feelings are not absolute; they are the play of our consciousness. If we meditate deeply, if we practise the precepts and gain insight into Reality, we shall understand the true nature of our minds, and see all these different feelings as they really are: nothing more than manifestations of the ever-changing flow of the conditioned mind. Then they will no longer dominate our lives.

Putting it at its simplest, Musō is reminding his friend of the Dharma, urging him to remember that his present experience, his present feelings, although they feel very absolute and imperative (he is locked into dealing with that drunken samurai who hit his friend and teacher), are impermanent. All mundane things are unsatisfactory, insubstantial, ungraspable, and they will pass. Bearing this in mind, he need not feel compelled to act on them.

Thus we can work on our feelings by recollecting the nature of phenomena, and applying that understanding to the situation in which we find ourselves. This approach can give us a broader and lighter perspective, sometimes even a glimpse of another dimension, which enables us to become free from being trapped in our limited views.

### Freedom for Others

It is appropriate that this book about freedom should end with a story of compassion and forgiveness. Zen being a Mahāyāna school, Musō has based his life on the Bodhisattva ideal. He is committed to gaining the total freedom of Enlightenment not for his own sake but out of the wish to help all living beings. This is how it has to be, for it is not possible to gain complete freedom for yourself alone. As long as we are still emotionally clenched around an idea of a fixed self which will become free, that limited notion will give us at best a limited freedom. It is only when we see through our belief that we are a fixed inherently-existing 'I' that we shall open our hearts finally and for ever to all life. It is that radical reorientation of our entire being which is the key to total freedom.

Whilst it may take us many years of work to arrive at that radical reorientation, it is good if from the beginning we work with the aim of becoming free in order to help others. After all, the world needs whatever crumbs of freedom we can feed it. We have only to look around us to see that there are many equivalents of the drunken samurai around today. There are plenty of people who have no notion that there could be a path to freedom. There are more than enough people trapped in painful mental states, who take them as absolute, as 'how life is'. These reflections can motivate us to put more energy into our own efforts to become freer, to work with our own minds, to create a gap of awareness in which we make new, creative choices. The whole world thirsts for freedom. Any step we can take along the path to liberation will be of benefit not just to ourselves alone. It will be a gift to the world.

# Conclusion

Although life may not be fair, it does offer us a great opportunity. We have the chance to follow the path to liberation, to whatever degree we wish. We can live ethical lives. We can practise meditation. We can develop wisdom and compassion. Then we shall be more than equal to anything that life can throw at us, as we have seen with many of the individuals in these stories.

This is a book of stories rather than a systematic presentation of the path to freedom. Nevertheless, through taking the stories to heart we should be able to discern a clear path of development, which if followed will lead us to liberation. In the first two chapters we encountered two people who could not bear to look at their true situation. Kisā Gotamī could not acknowledge that her child had died, but in her search for medicine she had the good fortune to be directed to the Buddha. By a kind stratagem he led her to see the distinction between the noble and the ignoble quests. Realizing that mundane life can never give fulfilment, she went for Refuge. This is the vital commitment to the path that we all need to make if we are to find true freedom, a commitment that underpins all our efforts. In Kisā Gotamī's case, so clear was her vision of the nature of existence when she went for Refuge that – unusually – she almost immediately gained Stream-entry, the point at which continued progress on the path to freedom becomes guaranteed.

Having made a commitment to freedom, we next need to establish an ethical basis for our practice. In the tragic story of Donald Crowhurst, who could not bring himself to acknowledge his true position even to those who cared about him, we witnessed the negative effects of ignoring the ethical dimension of life. We also saw that the Buddha's ethical precepts are not arbitrary rules, but the condensed wisdom, based on his Enlightened experience, of how to act in accordance with the true nature of things. Going with the grain of life in this way, we can avoid causing suffering to ourselves and others. Acting in the way that would come naturally to someone who is totally free, we become freer ourselves.

The positive and expansive mental states we produce by following the precepts are deepened through the practice of meditation. This involves exploring the depths of ourselves, as the King and his spiritual friend Jīvaka did symbolically by venturing into the forest, where they discovered the charmed circle of the Buddha and his silent meditating wanderers. We saw that this exploration requires us to let go of fixed ideas about who we are, and especially of seeing the world in terms of status and fixed roles.

The whole process of ethical practice and meditation involves overcoming our habitual tendencies to respond to stimuli with craving and aversion. This is true internally, in working directly with our own minds in meditation. It is also true in relation to our life as social beings in the wider world. In the last of our Pāli stories the jealous wanderers of other sects caused the people of Sāvatthi to unjustly accuse the Buddhists of murder. We saw the Buddha urging his followers not to respond in kind but to practise patience. Out of this we explored the whole tendency that underpins so much of mundane life, and binds us to the wheel of suffering – the tendency to think in terms of reciprocal relationships.

In examining that story, I made the point that the Buddha was not just recommending patient forbearance to his followers, but a dynamic loving-kindness, even towards those who were attacking them. This loving-kindness finds its fruition in the Mahāyāna ideal of the Bodhisattva, which is central to all forms of Tibetan Buddhism. When Dola Jigme Kalzang gave his life to prevent a total stranger from being tortured to death, he was expressing the heartfelt compassion for all that lives which is the hallmark of the Bodhisattva.

As we saw, this opening of the heart can be developed by meditation. It is born along with transcendental wisdom, which sees through the illusion of a separate, inherently-existent self. With the death of this illusion, you stand shoulder to shoulder with all life.

With the arising of wisdom and compassion, true freedom is established. When you have overcome all fear of death, and your heart is open to all beings, you are liberated. So the remainder of the stories all widened our understanding of the nature of that freedom, and how to attain it.

Nāropa's meeting with the strange old woman, who turned out to be the ḍākinī Vajrayoginī, showed us the dangers of settling down on the path to freedom. Sometimes we can even take ways of thinking and practices that are designed to help us become free, and wrap them around ourselves like new chains. So we were reminded of how the Dharma is a raft, that it is only a support on the way to freedom. We also looked at some pitfalls inherent in the ways we use language: bending our experience to conform to our language, treating abstractions as things, and taking life for granted by treating descriptions as explanations. All these are attempts to fix our experience, and prevent us from entering the ungraspable mystery of true freedom symbolized by the ḍākinī.

This theme was continued when we met Nāropa again, years later, when his disciple Marpa came to visit him, bearing the precious gift he had carried with him across the Himalayas. As the two men sat in their golden clearing, they showed us how we tend to become fixated on experience, and particularly how our limitless consciousness becomes trapped by our identification with the physical body.

We then moved on to Japan, where the Zen school has always emphasized teaching by example rather than explanation. Thus each of our three Zen masters demonstrated an aspect of freedom, under the most difficult circumstances possible. Challenged by life, they moved freely within an extra dimension, even when there appeared to be no room for manoeuvre in their external situation. Takuan demonstrated freedom from fear and hesitation. He went to face a tiger without a second thought, happily running down to its cage when most of us would hesitate, convinced we were going to our death.

Bokusan showed us his freedom from accepting the world on its own terms. Usually we take the world on the terms we are given. As a result, we feel constrained by our social situation and our relationships with people. Bokusan was not limited by the assumptions of the people around him. Three men said 'Do this, or we'll kill you,' and he was still free.

Musō returned us to the theme of Chapter 3. He was free from any desire to cause harm to anyone in any circumstances, even when he had been given very good reason. He had been hit with an iron weapon, and he would probably have a scar on his forehead until he died, but he did not react with anger or any desire for revenge. He kept a steady feeling of concern for everyone on the ferry, even the drunken samurai. Through exploring his teaching to his friend (through which Musō saved the samurai's life), we saw ways of containing and working with our own powerful negative emotions and impulses.

Throughout this book we have seen many demonstrations of the wonderful potential of the human spirit. To take just a few examples, we witnessed a woman, crazed with grief and feeling she had nothing to live for, transformed into a serene sage. We watched a man submitting himself to a painful death in order to save a complete stranger, a thief, from suffering. We saw a human being leap into a tiger's cage without a second thought. These three people were not born with the ability to act in these ways. They developed it through meditation and Dharma practice. All men and women have the potential to become heroes and heroines of wisdom and compassion.

To help us fulfil that potential, we can store these incidents away in our hearts and allow them to affect us. We can live in them for a while in our imagination, and allow them to change our lives. These stories can help us to remember to dwell in the gap of awareness between stimulus and response, making efforts to transform ourselves, recalling Musō's injunction, 'Now, now is the time to apply our Buddhism.' If we keep doing this, we shall eventually find that these stories have helped to ferry us across to the further shore of freedom.

# NOTES AND REFERENCES

1  In order to compress the unfolding drama of Donald Crowhurst's
   eight-and-a-half months at sea into a few pages, I have slightly altered
   the chronology of one or two incidents. I have not changed any of the
   facts. For a full account of this story see Nicholas Tomalin and Ron
   Hall, *The Strange Voyage of Donald Crowhurst*, Book Society, London
   1970.

2  Bhikkhu Ñāṇamoli (trans.), *Majjhima-Nikāya* 36.

3  Steven Collins, in his Introduction to the *Therīgāthā*, published as
   C.A.F. Rhys Davids and K.R. Norman (trans.), *Poems of Early Buddhist
   Nuns*, Pali Text Society, Oxford 1989.

4  There is a legend that Gotamī was married to the son of a merchant
   because after he had fallen on hard times she acted as a lucky charm to
   restore his fortune. See E.W. Burlingame, *A Treasury of Buddhist Stories*,
   Buddhist Publication Society, Kandy 1996, p.213.

5  The verses from the *Therīgāthā* in this chapter are my own adaptations
   based on C.A.F. Rhys Davids' translation. For a useful discussion of the
   verses attributed to Kisā Gotamī in the *Therīgāthā*, see Susan Murcott,
   *The First Buddhist Women*, Parallax, Berkeley 1991, pp.84–8.

6  A sutta is one of the thousands of recorded discourses of the Buddha
   (or, occasionally, one of his Enlightened disciples) that make up a large
   part of the Pāli canonical texts. The sutta referred to here is the
   *Ariyapariyesana Sutta* from the *Majjhima-Nikāya* of the Pāli Canon.

7  In Tibetan Buddhist ritual, much of which was imported from India,
   mustard seed is used for expelling 'hindering demons', including
   curing the diseases they may cause (see Dagyab Rinpoche, *Buddhist*

*Symbols in Tibetan Culture*, Wisdom, Boston 1995, pp.58–60). So it is possible that mustard was used for magical purposes to cure disease in ancient India.

8 The story of Gotamī's breakthrough to insight while watching a flickering lamp is told in the *Dhammapada* commentary. A reference to it can be found in Narada Thera, *The Dhammapada – a Translation*, BMS 1978, p.108.

9 See *Sāmaññaphala Sutta* in Maurice Walshe (trans.), *The Long Discourses of the Buddha*, Wisdom, Boston 1995, pp.91 *et seq.*

10 *Udāna* II.x. in F.L. Woodward (trans.), *The Minor Anthologies of the Pali Canon*, Pali Text Society, Oxford 1935, pp.23–4.

11 For this story see Paul Reps, *Zen Flesh, Zen Bones*, Penguin, London 1991, p.40.

12 This story is told in *Udāna* IV.viii, op. cit., pp.52–4.

13 *Kakacūpama Sutta, Majjhima-Nikāya* 21.

14 *Dhammapada*, chapter 1, verse 5.

15 *Bodhisattva* and *Arhant* are Sanskrit. The Pāli forms are *Bodhisatta* and *Arahant* or *Arahat*.

16 *Vinaya* i.21, trans. F.L. Woodward, in *Some Sayings of the Buddha*, Buddhist Society, London 1973, p.22.

17 The Marquess of Halifax (1633–95), 'Of Punishment' in his *Political Thoughts and Reflections*.

18 For a clear and practical introduction to loving-kindness meditation, see chapter 2 of Kamalashila, *Meditation – The Buddhist Way of Tranquillity and Insight*, Windhorse, Birmingham 1996.

19 There are many books available on Tibetan Buddhism which describe one or both of these methods. Here are a couple of examples, drawn from different schools of Tibetan Buddhism: Geshe Wangchen, *Awakening the Mind of Enlightenment*, Wisdom, London 1987; and Patrul Rinpoche, *The Words of My Perfect Teacher*, trans. Padmakara Translation Group, HarperCollins, San Francisco 1994.

20 What we know of Dola Jigme Kalzang's life is summarized in Tulku Thondup, *Masters of Meditation and Miracles – The Longchen Nyingthig Lineage of Tibetan Buddhism*, Shambhala, Boston 1966, pp.173–4. The story of his death on the copper horse is also told in Surya Das, *The Snow Lion's Turquoise Mane – Wisdom Tales From Tibet*, Harper, San Francisco 1992, pp.234–5.

21 Herbert V. Guenther (trans.), *The Life and Teaching of Nāropa*, OUP, New York 1971, pp.21–2.

22 Ibid. p.24.

23 I have borrowed most of my comments on the Dharma as raft from an article I wrote for the *FWBO Newsletter* no.32, Autumn 1976, p.5.

24 C.W. Nichol, *Moving Zen – Karate as a Way to Gentleness*, Bodley Head, London 1975.

25 Vessantara, *Meeting the Buddhas – A Guide to Buddhas, Bodhisattvas, and Tantric Deities*, Windhorse, Birmingham 1998. See chapter 23, 'Dancing in the Sky'.

26 *The Life and Teaching of Nāropa*, op. cit., p.26.

27 Milarepa became perhaps the best-known of all the meditation practitioners of Tibet. See Lobsang P. Lhalungpa, *The Life of Milarepa*, Shambhala, Boston and London 1977, and Garma C.C. Chang (trans.), *The Hundred Thousand Songs of Milarepa* (2 vols.), Shambhala, Boulder 1962.

28 There are different versions of the incident with the gold. See for instance *The Life and Teaching of Nāropa*, op. cit., p.105, and Tsang Nyon Heruka, *The Life of Marpa the Translator* trans. Nalanda Translation Committee, Prajna, Boulder 1982, p.87.

29 *The Tibetan Book of the Dead* is the popular English title of the book known in Tibetan as the *Bardo Thödol*. There are several translations available in English, including those by Fremantle and Trungpa, Shambhala, Boulder 1975, and Robert A.F. Thurman, Aquarian/Thorsons, London 1994.

30 This verse is attributed to Bodhidharma, the First Patriarch of Zen in China, but was actually formulated during the T'ang period. See Heinrich Dumoulin, *Zen Buddhism: A History, vol.1: India and China*, Macmillan, New York 1994, pp.85 and 102, note 1.

31 Trevor Leggett, *The Tiger's Cave – Translations of Japanese Zen Texts*, Routledge and Kegan Paul, London 1977. For the story of Takuan and the tiger, see pp.159–60. Hirose (see Note 34 below) describes this story as a legend, whilst Leggett relates it as fact. Certainly there are other true stories which Hirose tells of Takuan that present him as completely fearless and spontaneous. For instance, in one story he seeks out and overcomes three armed bandits using only his priest's staff (*nyoi*) (Hirose, pp.77–83).

32 The Shōgun Iemitsu lived from 1623 to 1651. If we assume that Iemitsu was 20 at this time, then Takuan would have been about 70 and Yagyū a couple of years older.

33 This scroll by Kishi Ganku (1749–1838) is in the British Museum – classified as Japanese Painting ADD79.

34 For details of Takuan's life and writings see Heinrich Dumoulin, *Zen Buddhism: A History, vol. 2: Japan* Macmillan, New York 1990, pp.274–88. For a compilation of his teachings see Nobuko Hirose (compiler and trans.), *Immovable Wisdom*, Element, Shaftesbury, Dorset 1992.

35 D.T. Suzuki (trans.), *Essays in Zen Buddhism (Third Series)*, Rider, London 1970, pp.362–4.

36 *The Tiger's Cave*, op. cit., p.161.

37 The full list, known as the six perfections, consists of generosity, ethics, patience, energy, meditation, and wisdom.

38 *The Tiger's Cave*, op. cit., p.161.

39 Chinese whispers is the game known as 'telephone' in the USA.

40 *The Tiger's Cave*, op. cit., p.163.

41 For an account of Musō's life and teaching see Heinrich Dumoulin, *Zen Buddhism: A History, vol.2: Japan*, op. cit., pp.153–69.

42 Musō Kokushi, *Dream Conversations – on Buddhism and Zen*, trans. Thomas Cleary, Shambhala, Boston and London 1996.

# INDEX

*viparyāsas* 34f
visualization 125

**W**
wanderers 53, 63
Watts, Alan 171
wholeheartedness 113
wine 150
wisdom 109, 127
words 101, 103ff, 109, 116,
    *see also* communication

word transmission 116
worldly winds 14ff

**Y**
Yagyū 135, 140
Yasodharā 33

**Z**
zazen 133
Zen 117, 133, 135, 136, 149,
    *see also* Obaku, Rinzai, Sōtō

The Windhorse symbolizes the energy of the enlightened mind carrying the Three Jewels – the Buddha, the Dharma, and the Sangha – to all sentient beings.

Buddhism is one of the fastest-growing spiritual traditions in the Western world. Throughout its 2,500-year history, it has always succeeded in adapting its mode of expression to suit whatever culture it has encountered.

Windhorse Publications aims to continue this tradition as Buddhism comes to the West. Today's Westerners are heirs to the entire Buddhist tradition, free to draw instruction and inspiration from all the many schools and branches. Windhorse publishes works by authors who not only understand the Buddhist tradition but are also familiar with Western culture and the Western mind. Manuscripts welcome.

For orders and catalogues contact

| WINDHORSE PUBLICATIONS | WINDHORSE BOOKS | WEATHERHILL INC |
| 11 PARK ROAD | P O BOX 574 | 41 MONROE TURNPIKE |
| BIRMINGHAM | NEWTOWN | TRUMBULL |
| B13 8AB | NSW 2042 | CT 06611 |
| UK | AUSTRALIA | USA |

Windhorse Publications is an arm of the Friends of the Western Buddhist Order, which has more than sixty centres on five continents. Through these centres, members of the Western Buddhist Order offer regular programmes of events for the general public and for more experienced students. These include meditation classes, public talks, study on Buddhist themes and texts, and 'bodywork' classes such as t'ai chi, yoga, and massage. The FWBO also runs several retreat centres and the Karuna Trust, a fund-raising charity that supports social welfare projects in the slums and villages of India.

Many FWBO centres have residential spiritual communities and ethical businesses associated with them. Arts activities are encouraged too, as is the development of strong bonds of friendship between people who share the same ideals. In this way the FWBO is developing a unique approach to Buddhism, not simply as a set of techniques, less still as an exotic cultural interest, but as a creatively directed way of life for people living in the modern world.

If you would like more information about the FWBO please visit www.fwbo.org or write to

LONDON BUDDHIST CENTRE
51 ROMAN ROAD
LONDON
E2 0HU
UK

ARYALOKA
HEARTWOOD CIRCLE
NEWMARKET
NH 03857
USA

# ALSO FROM WINDHORSE

VESSANTARA

## THE MANDALA OF THE FIVE BUDDHAS

The mandala of the Five Buddhas is an important Buddhist symbol – a multi-faceted jewel communicating the different aspects of Enlightenment. Meeting each Buddha in turn, we start to awaken to the qualities they embody – energy, beauty, love, confidence, and freedom.

By contemplating the mandala as a whole we can transform ourselves through the power of the imagination, and experience the majesty of the mind set free.

*96 pages, with colour plates*
*ISBN 1 899579 16 8*
*£5.99/$11.95*

VESSANTARA

## MEETING THE BUDDHAS:

## A GUIDE TO BUDDHAS, BODHISATTVAS, AND TANTRIC DEITIES

Sitting poised and serene upon fragrant lotus blooms, they offer smiles of infinite tenderness, immeasurable wisdom. Bellowing formidable roars of angry triumph from the heart of blazing infernos, they dance on the naked corpses of their enemies.

Who are these beings – the Buddhas, Bodhisattvas, and Protectors, the 'angry demons' and 'benign deities' – of the Buddhist Tantric tradition? Are they products of an alien, even disturbed, imagination? Or are they, perhaps, real? What have they got to do with Buddhism? And what have they got to do with us?

In this vivid informed account, an experienced Western Buddhist guides us into the heart of this magical realm and introduces us to the miraculous beings who dwell there.

*368 pages, with text illustrations and colour plates*
*ISBN 0 904766 53 5*
*£14.99/$29.95*

PARAMANANDA

CHANGE YOUR MIND: A PRACTICAL GUIDE TO BUDDHIST MEDITATION

Buddhism is based on the truth that, with effort, we can change the way we are. But how? Among the many methods Buddhism has to offer, meditation is the most direct. It is the art of getting to know one's own mind and learning to encourage what is best in us.

This is an approachable and thorough guide to meditation, based on traditional material but written in a light and modern style. Colourfully illustrated with anecdotes and tips from the author's experience as a meditator and teacher, it also offers refreshing inspiration to seasoned meditators.

*208 pages, with photographs*
*ISBN 0 904766 81 0*
*£8.99/$17.95*


BODHIPAKSA

VEGETARIANISM

Part of a series on *Living a Buddhist Life*, this book explores connections between vegetarianism and the spiritual life.

As a trained vet, Bodhipaksa is well placed to reveal the suffering of animals in the farming industry, and as a practising Buddhist he can identify the ethical consequences of inflicting such suffering. Through the Buddhist teaching of interconnectedness he lays bare the effects our eating habits can have upon us, upon animals, and upon the environment.

He concludes that by becoming vegetarian we can affirm life in a very clear and immediate way, and so experience a greater sense of contentment, harmony, and happiness.

*112 pages*
*ISBN 1 899579 15 X*
*£4.99/$9.95*

JINANANDA

**MEDITATING**

This is a guide to Buddhist meditation that is in sympathy with modern lifestyle. Accessible and thought-provoking, this books tells you what you need to know to get started with meditation, and keep going through the ups and downs of everyday life. Realistic, witty, and very inspiring.

*136 pages*
*ISBN 1 899579 07 9*
*£4.99/$9.95*

SANGHARAKSHITA

**THE BODHISATTVA IDEAL:**

**WISDOM AND COMPASSION IN BUDDHISM**

How can we live an ideal life in the real world? How can we be happy and at the same time responsive to the sufferings of others? It can be done: this is the message of the Bodhisattva Ideal.

Sangharakshita places one of the sublimest ideals mankind has ever seen within the context of the entire Buddhist tradition. Unfolding this vision of our potential, he demonstrates how we ourselves can faithfully engage with that vision and make our lives worthwhile.

*256 pages*
*ISBN 1 899579 20 6*
*£9.99/$19.95*

DAVID SMITH

## A RECORD OF AWAKENING: PRACTICE AND INSIGHT ON THE BUDDHIST PATH

*A Record of Awakening* is the remarkable fruit of more than twenty years' immersion in Buddhist practice: a practice that has been both deep and far-reaching.

In this book, David Smith, 'an ordinary working-class chap' who came across Buddhism, shares his extraordinary inner experience. Taking us through his journey – from initial practice in the Zen tradition and three years as a Theravadin monk to his recent years as a lay practitioner in East London – he describes the basic principles of his practice and the process whereby the 'tap root of ignorance' is cut and the Awakened Mind is born.

*160 pages*
*ISBN 1 899579 18 4*
*£7.99/$15.95*

TEJANANDA

## THE BUDDHIST PATH TO AWAKENING

The word Buddha means 'one who is awake'. In this accessible introduction, Tejananda alerts us to the Buddha's wake-up call, illustrating how the Buddhist path can help us develop a clearer mind and a more compassionate heart.

Drawing on over twenty years' of Buddhist meditation and study, Tejananda gives us a straightforward and encouraging description of the path of the Buddha and his followers – the path that leads ultimately to our own 'awakening'.

*224 pages, with diagrams*
*ISBN 1 899579 02 8*
*£8.99/$17.95*

SARA HAGEL (EDITOR)

## DHARDO RIMPOCHE: A CELEBRATION

This book is a celebration of the life and work of Dhardo Rimpoche, one of Sangharakshita's main teachers.

Dhardo Rimpoche was revered in his own lifetime as a living Bodhisattva. These reminiscences from his disciples in the East, and his adopted disciples in the West, reveal again and again his perfection of the qualities of selflessness, generosity, kindness, and mindfulness.

*128 pages with black & white photos*
*ISBN 1 899579 26 5*
*£9.99/$19.95*

## METTA: THE PRACTICE OF LOVING KINDNESS

Metta, or loving kindness, lies at the heart of Buddhism. It is kindness at its purest and strongest, a loving response to all life – with no strings attached. In this book, seven experienced meditators share their reflections on the nature of metta, giving instruction and advice on its cultivation. This traditional meditation practice can help us to transform our emotional life into one consistently based on love.

*80 pages*
*ISBN 0 904766 99 3*
*£4.99/$9.95*

# BOOKS FOR CHILDREN

Three magical tales from the Buddhist tradition, beautifully illustrated and retold by Adiccabandhu and Padmasri in a style that will delight the young reader.

## THE MONKEY KING

A stirring jungle tale of greed, heroism, and mangoes.

*32 pages fully illustrated in colour*
*ISBN 1 899579 09 5*
*£5.99/$11.95*

## SIDDHARTHA AND THE SWAN

Quarrelling over a wounded swan, the young Prince Siddhartha helps his cousin learn about kindness to animals.

*32 pages fully illustrated in colour*
*ISBN 1 899579 10 9*
*£5.99/$11.95*

## THE LION AND THE JACKAL

A community of lions and jackals learns that friendship is built on trust and generosity.

*32 pages fully illustrated in colour*
*ISBN 1 899579 13 3*
*£5.99/$11.95*